CONQUERING CHALLENGES

A Working Mother's Story

CONQUERING   CHALLENGES

A Working Mother's Story

by

Elizabeth Blake, MT ASCP

Author's Note

A factual account of my years working in the medical field, I wrote, *"Conquering Challenges: A Working Mother's Story"* in honest faith to the best of my recollection.

The names of most of my co-workers and the hospital in Phoenix, Arizona have been changed to protect their privacy. In rare instances, two people have been rolled into one character. Although all events are true, they are not necessarily all presented chronologically, in order to facilitate the flow of the story.

Dedication

This book is dedicated to all the working mothers and fathers, who juggle work demands with parenting.

And to all the healthcare workers who dedicate their lives to helping people.

Acknowledgements

I'd like to thank all my critique partners who helped me with this work. Kathy, Nikki, Sandy, Toby, Michael, Cherie. You are great!

Thank you Travis Miles for the great cover.

I wish to thank my family for being the best.

I'd like to thank my friends—Kathy T, Jennifer, Nancy Jo, Marsha, Liz, Linda—who never stopped supporting me.

And lastly I want to especially thank my parents, who were there for me when I needed them.

Thank you, all of you.

PART ONE
DECISIONS

"We have to get Amy out of the Anderson's house right now!" my mother said. The frantic look on her face and tone of her voice alarmed me.

"What's going on?" I asked. The Andersons were a nice, Christian couple with two little boys. They had a sweet babysitter who had some physical challenges but was capable of also watching my five-month-old infant Amy while I commuted to college. The Andersons had suggested we share babysitting services, saying their sitter could use some extra money. They were happy to have Amy at their home during the day. They were gone at work anyway.

"Because I just heard that they have hired an attorney to draw up papers. They're planning to adopt Amy!" My mother paced our linoleum kitchen floor.

What on earth? Where would they get the idea it was okay to take my child? Without even asking me or discussing it with me? "That doesn't make any sense," I said, trying to hold in my anger. "What makes them think they can do that?"

"Evidently Mrs. Anderson is Rh negative and is afraid of not being able to have any more children and she wants a girl."

I guess the fact that I also was Rh negative didn't factor into Mrs. Anderson's plans. Or that I was the one who had given birth to Amy. Or that I didn't plan to give my own child to anyone else. My shoulders slumped. I closed my eyes and rubbed my temples. When would it ever end? Ever since I became pregnant, there had been somebody somewhere plotting to take my child away from

1

me. I jumped into my parent's car and quickly drove to the Anderson's farm just ten miles from my parent's home in southern Minnesota. I was twenty years old. It was February, 1970.

As I navigated the country roads through the snow and freezing cold weather, my anger boiled to the surface. How dare those people assume they could take my baby without even discussing it with me? Just because I was a single mother? This gave them automatic rights to my child?

How much more could I take? I'd had enough of lawyers by then. Amy's biological father's lawyer had sent me letters while I was pregnant, trying to bargain out of child support, denying his client was the father, and threatening to interview people at my college to "see who else I'd been sleeping with." The answer to that was a resounding "nobody else," but just the idea of those interviews had been upsetting to me and my parents. That lawyer offered me "Two hundred dollars to forget the whole thing." Yes, I was sick of lawyers.

I was also sick of ministers after my sister's pastor told me, "Jesus will forgive you of your sin *IF* you give your child up for adoption." Fortunately, my faith in God's love for me was stronger than that. My own minister hadn't been any help. And Amy's paternal grandfather was a minister who wanted me to give her up for adoption.

I felt bad for Amy's physically challenged babysitter. She had grown fond of Amy in the month she had been watching her. Fortunately, the Andersons were both at work and I didn't have to confront them. I was able to sit and visit with the babysitter for a while. It wasn't her fault. My mother called the Andersons later and said we would make other arrangements.

We found a different sitter right next door to my parents' home as I continued to commute to college, where I was a junior, one hour away in Mankato, MN. Later, I moved to Mankato and brought Amy with me, finding a sitter there.

One freezing day I had to take Amy on an errand. Returning home, I got off the bus to walk the one block to our Mankato apartment. The wind blew fierce and deathly cold. I struggled to take in a breath against the cruel gusts. I held Amy wrapped in a blanket against my body and buried her head in my chest, praying she could breathe. Even turning around and walking backwards didn't escape the biting gale. It surrounded us. I made it to our apartment, unnerved but safe. We lived there for two years.

Amy was a friendly and active toddler. One day I walked out of the bathroom to find my lipstick smeared all over the walls, baby powder covering the rug, burners on the gas stove all turned on, and the apartment door wide open. In just the two minutes I was in the bathroom. Thoughts of kidnappers whirled through my brain as I burst out the door and ran down the hallway of the apartment building calling, "Amy!"

Turned out, she had gone to a neighbor's apartment and knocked on the door. The occupant had opened her door and saw no one, until she glanced down and there stood Amy. My daughter toddled in, plopped herself in a chair, and asked for a cookie.

That's how I met Linda. Linda loved kids and thought Amy was adorable. We became good friends and kept in touch after we graduated and both moved.

I finished college the summer of 1971 with a degree in education and relocated to another small town in northern Iowa where I got a teaching job. I also found a nice two-bedroom place in a trailer park along Spirit Lake, Iowa—a beautiful lakeside area. A lovely woman across the road babysat while I went to work in a nearby country school just across the border in Minnesota.

To my frustration, a weird, overweight man frequently visited a neighbor of mine. One day, he saw Amy playing outside and pointed his stubby finger at her and laughed. "You're a mistake, did you know that?" My neighbor stood there with an amused look plastered on his face.

Amy was a plucky little two-year-old. She stomped her foot on the hard ground and defiantly replied, "I not a mittake!"

The man guffawed. I grabbed Amy and brought her inside, hugging her close. "Jesus loves you. Mommy loves you. Grandma loves you. Grandpa loves you..." We went through the whole list of my large family who loved her. I was one of six children and my three older sisters were all married. That always made Amy happy. She forgot about the incident in a couple minutes but I didn't. It burned inside me, waiting to erupt .

That evening, after Amy fell asleep, I marched over to my neighbor's place and pounded on the door. "You keep that weirdo friend of yours away from my daughter, do you hear? If I ever see him near her again, I'll call the police. Understand?"

He meekly nodded his head.

We didn't have any more problems after that but the next school year, I found a different place to live—on the second floor of an apartment building in a small Minnesota town.

The winters were a challenge as I struggled to get to work. One cold morning while standing at the top of the staircase, I observed the flight of steps below me. With Amy bundled in my right arm, I tried to balance her as I held onto the railing with my left hand. She wore a bulky winter coat with mittens clipped to the end of its sleeves, over a warm shirt and knit pants and tights. Her winter hat was tied with a bow under her chin. Fortunately her snow pants and rubber boots were kept at that babysitter's house for playtime, or she would have been even bulkier.

Carefully, I made my way down the stairs to my car, praying my new Ford Maverick would start in this freezing weather. I didn't have anywhere to plug in an engine heater. Even inside the building, my breath steamed like cold little clouds. As I descended the staircase, my purse slipped off my left shoulder landing inside my elbow, yanking me off balance. At the same instant, my shoe slipped on some melted snow on the step.

With a yelp, I lurched forward onto my knees. Boom, boom, boom, my whole body bounced down the entire staircase on my knees. *Oh no! Amy's legs will get caught under me and break!* Helpless, I tried to stop my fall but couldn't. All I could do was hang on tight to Amy so she didn't fall head first.

We fell all the way to the bottom. Heart racing and gasping for breath, I frantically felt Amy's legs. Nothing seemed broken. She wasn't crying and appeared okay. It was only then I noticed my own pain.

Huge holes gaped in my navy blue tights, exposing my bloodied scraped knees. The pain throbbed but I knew I was lucky it hadn't been worse. My skirt was undamaged but I'd have to clean my wounds and change my tights before I went to work.

My car did start that day but I began to think about moving to a warmer climate. Minnesota winters were tough for me as a single mother, even though I'd been born and raised there.

The menacing weather wasn't the only reason I thought of moving. I also wanted a larger city—someplace where I could escape small town judgment.. Although my parents, friends, family, and my parents' friends were supportive, I found resistance and judgment from social workers, counselors, ministers, former teachers, even strangers. The town newspaper refused to list her baptism in the paper in their "Baptisms section." It was time for a different environment.

After that, things occurred to point me in a certain direction. Someone up there was watching out for us.

I needed to find my professional passion in life. I had two requirements. What did I love doing? And what would pay enough to support the two of us? Without child support, making a decent salary was an important consideration. The little bit of money my lawyer wrenched from her father that I got in a small lump sum all went toward paying some medical bills.

I loved being a mother. How could God bless me so much? He gave me an adorable child whom I cherished with all my heart. Somehow He saw fit to fill my life with tremendous joy and I felt humbled. My heart told me God would be Amy's father and always look after her. Couldn't get a better father than that and I knew we'd be fine. God's strong presence was always in our lives.

Linda had moved to Hawaii. We were both twenty-three and restless. She suggested I join her. I mulled the idea in the back of my mind. Letters from Linda sounded glamorous. I felt a tug toward that paradise across the sea.

I didn't miss her father or have any feelings of desire for him anymore. Those feelings had long ago vanished. Bitterness and resentment churned inside of me however because his last words he ever said to me were, "I think you should give the child up for adoption." That was before she was born. It seemed like most of society wanted me to give her away. That's what I resented. It would've broken my heart but he didn't care as he walked away. I had buried all those thoughts deep inside me where they could

5

barely be reached.

I became very good at shoving down my feelings. I never discussed those feelings with anyone and knew I had to get away and leave it all behind me. For my own emotional health.

I kept in touch with Linda through letters. I wanted the chance to explore a little bit of the world before Amy entered school. Once that happened, I'd need to settle down into one place. I didn't want her changing schools any more than absolutely necessary.

I began considering moving to Hawaii and searching for a career that would fulfill my two requirements. By the time Amy was three-and-a-half I had made my decision.

With a grateful heart, my savings, and my parents' blessing, I took my daughter's small hand, left Minnesota's cold winter and flew to Hawaii. I planned to stay there just one year. Then I'd return to Minnesota and settle down into a professional career in one place so she wouldn't need to switch schools when she got older. That was my deadline—one year—to find my professional passion. There were some good memories in Minnesota of course. I would need to focus on the good and bury the bad forever. This would take time but it sounded like a good plan.

As the two of us flew over the Pacific on our way to the islands, I pointed out the window. "Amy, look outside at the clouds."

She looked out and up, not seeing anything but blue sky. "Where?"

"Look down, they're below us."

Amy glanced down and looked alarmed. Panicking, her eyes popped wide open. "Mommy! The kwouds fell down!"

I laughed. "No, honey, we're above them!" In my excitement over our adventure together, I indeed felt above the clouds.

Amy making a snowman in our front yard in MN.

Me holding Amy, with my brother-in-law,
the minister, and my sister Janice, at Amy's
baptism.

PART TWO
HAWAII

Linda invited us to stay with her and her roommates in a Waikiki apartment until I could find a place for Amy and me. My first morning in Hawaii in January, 1973 I awoke early, rose and gazed out the window. The sun shone brightly in the clear blue sky. What a difference from the Minnesota snowstorm we had flown out of. Palm trees lined the street and not far away, the ocean stretched endlessly. This was my first close glimpse of the Pacific. I'd never traveled before. Ever since Hawaii became a state when I was a child, the beauty and romance of these islands mesmerized me.

I quietly opened the sliding door and slipped onto the lanai. The clean, refreshing smell of saltwater infiltrated my nostrils as I breathed in the wonderment of Hawaii. Tilting my head toward the sun, I closed my eyes and smiled. Paradise for one whole year. Excitement filled me. I could barely wait to get to the beach but everyone else still slept. I screamed inside my head, "Wake up. I want to experience Hawaii!"

Linda was great. She and I didn't do drugs, though one of the roommates kept LSD in the refrigerator. Fearing Amy might get into it, I decided to move after a couple weeks and found an apartment of my own in a residential area. The extra rent dug deep into my savings but I knew it would have to be done sooner or later.

Amy and I helped each other as teammates in life. I can't count how many times we came out of the grocery store and I searched the parking lot, unable to find the old Volkswagen bug I purchased. Amy always remembered where we had parked. Being a mother was very rewarding for me and I thanked God every day for her. I met other mothers in my new apartment building and we babysat for each other. Amy made friends easily. Her friends were Japanese, Chinese, Polynesian, and Caucasian. Hawaii was a wonderful place for her to have this exposure.

My savings were running low so I quickly found a job as a camera girl, taking pictures of tourists while they sat waiting for resort shows to start. Other employees of the photography company developed the pictures during the shows. Then I sold them to the tourists after the shows finished.

One night I peeked into the lounge room of the Royal Hawaiian Hotel on Waikiki Beach. My company had asked another camera girl and me to take complimentary pictures of a group of celebrities as a good-will gesture to the hotel housing our small office. I had no idea who the celebrities would be.

The renowned Tahitian dancer Manu Bentley danced on stage. Peter Graves of Mission Impossible fame, and Mike Connors, famous for his Joe Mannix TV role, sat at a table with a third man and two women. The rest of the room sat empty. The third man turned his head slightly and I saw his unmistakable profile.

Clint Eastwood.

My heart raced so fast, it made me light-headed. *Don't faint now!* As a big-time-fan, I couldn't believe I was actually going to meet Clint Eastwood.

I stared in astonishment and grabbed the arm of my fellow camera girl to steady myself. I wanted to jump up and down and scream, "Clint Eastwood! Peter Graves and Mike Connors! Are you kidding me?" but I clamped my mouth shut. Clint looked gorgeous in his Hawaiian shirt and lei.

Drawing a deep breath, I stood up straight, smoothed my floor length cocktail dress, and floated into the room with my professional camera in hand. The celebrities talked among themselves and ate. Assuming an air of sophistication I didn't feel inside, I approached their table. The other camera girl and I smiled graciously and snapped pictures of the group. Surreal. Be professional, be adult, I reminded myself. I think I managed not to appear like a silly school girl but I'm not sure.

Mr. Eastwood excused himself and went to the men's room. He looked pretty shnockered and I suspected he got sick in there. After he returned, he was a perfect gentleman, sitting quietly with a friendly smile on his face.

I sidled next to him at the table so my comrade could take a picture of us. He kept looking at me with narrowed eyes and an inquisitive expression on his face. I couldn't tell if he was thinking, "Gee, she's kind of cute," or, "Wow, is she weird." I preferred to think the former.

Clint and I ate pupus—Hawaiian appetizers. We chatted for a short while—the "Hi, how are you" kind of chatter—until I suspected his wife wanted him all to herself. She must've been the most understanding woman on earth, since he had thousands of female fans around the world.

Overall, I loved that job—glamorous and fun. It enabled me to hang around various fancy hotels our photography company served and meet the performers. Yet it was just barely paying the bills.

For one year, Amy and I scraped along on my salary. Exploring the island, trips to the ocean, and making new friends made the time fly by. At the end of twelve months, a thought rammed through my head, "*Why go back to Minnesota?*" It was cold back there. Flashbacks of the fierce winters made me shiver in the sun.

But mostly, I wasn't ready emotionally to return—someday I would be, but not yet. I looked around at Paradise. Hawaii was a great place to raise a child because of its many different cultures, friendly people and the accepting Aloha Spirit. People in Hawaii didn't care I wasn't married. I knew I'd continue to miss my family in but the islands called to me in a convincing voice. I decided to stay in Hawaii for a while longer. And after a lot of deliberation, I still was no closer to finding my professional passion.

My parents visited us and I planned trips back to Minnesota for Amy and me to visit my family and friends. I missed my friends but we were scattered now, all of us trying to find our own way in our lives.

I evaluated my strengths and preferences. I needed a profession that offered jobs anywhere I chose to live in the future. With a surplus of teachers at that time, there were no teaching jobs available.

I had a considerable amount of science and math credits in my college background from Minnesota. Since I liked the sciences

I decided to pursue a degree in medical technology, which involved performing lab tests in a hospital or private laboratory. I only needed a handful of specific courses and some practical training. I was one of those people who enjoyed school. Working in the medical field would fulfill the desire I had to help people, challenge me mentally, pay the bills and allow me to meet like-minded people. The thought excited me and the more I contemplated it, the more passionate I felt. And there was always a need for medical personnel, wherever one lived.

An interest in science came naturally to me. My father obtained a degree in chemistry with a minor in zoology from the private college, Carleton, in my hometown. I grew up surrounded by science in our home. He had been a straight-A student in that academic college. He was also a five-star letterman in sports. Dad was a perfectionist and had very high standards. More than anything I yearned for my father, who taught general science and consumer math at the high school in my hometown, to be proud of me. He had always been a vivid force in my life. That was another reason why I chose the medical field. He and I were alike in many ways.

I enrolled in medical technology classes offered at a nearby beautiful campus overlooking Diamond Head. Wanting to be home at night, I took a job as a part-time on-campus secretary with flexible hours. I hated leaving Amy for any length of time, but it was necessary for our financial future.

Even though we had very little money, I made sure Amy always ate nutritious meals. For breakfast she had Malt-O-Meal hot cereal with milk. It calculated to seven cents a serving. Her school lunches cost twenty-five cents. For dinner, I made sure she had a fruit, a vegetable, the island's ubiquitous rice and a glass of milk. I ate the same. I couldn't afford meat. We scrimped, but it worked. We lived in a tiny studio apartment and managed on very little. It was only a temporary situation until I could get a full-time, higher paying job in a hospital laboratory.

I didn't want to sit around waiting for Prince Charming to rescue me. My motto in life was, and always has been, "Do your best. Let God do the rest." I knew as long as I tried to make a living, God would always help the two of us.

Although meeting a nice handsome doctor wouldn't exactly

have been against my religion.

***

The Diamond Head campus vista displayed lush greenery, tall swaying palm trees, and in the distance, the blue ocean splashed against black rocks. Some of the college's buildings had been barracks built during WWII. The college transformed them into classrooms and labs with desks and tables, sinks and faucets. I liked the sense of history there as I went to class.

The view plus the history gave the campus a sentimental feeling. I stood on top of the hill, surrounded by tropical foliage and felt the wind on my face. Tall palm trees swayed in the breeze. I smiled at the sun and breathed in the distant scent of fresh salt air. How I loved that aroma. I felt at peace.

I needed clinical chemistry, diagnostic microbiology, hematology, immunology, and immuno-hematology—blood banking—just five courses. Very do-able. I already had all the other sciences and math the medical technology program required.

In those classes I met another student, Liz, who was Chinese-American on her father's side and English-American on her mother's. She had long brown hair and attractive Eurasian features. In one of our first conversations I said, "I've had a crush on James Shigeta ever since I saw him in the movie Flower Drum Song when I was little." The fact that a haole—Caucasian—on the mainland liked James Shigeta back in the fifties blazed the way for many other discussions and we became close friends.

During a microbiology lab, Liz pulled me into the hallway, her dark eyes wide with a frantic look. Her slim fingers dug into my skin as she gripped my arm.

What the heck? Were we flunking the class? Was the program closing down? Or something worse? I gritted my teeth, waiting for whatever bad news she had.

She leaned toward me and whispered in a conspiratorial tone, "Hey! Did you know we're going to have to work with poop?"

Where did she get a nutty idea like that? I was sure she was out of her mind. "No," I answered. "No way."

"It's true! Tori just told me! We have to test fecal material!"

"I don't believe it. We only have to test blood and urine."

12

Urine was bad enough. And I liked looking in a microscope differentiating blood cell morphology. That was interesting. But feces? Yuck. She must be mistaken. I enjoyed the mental stimulation of learning medical technology, but please, we had to draw the line somewhere!

She nodded her head. "Tori knows someone who works in a lab in Pearl City. She tests poop all the time. For abnormal bacteria, worms, blood, whatever."

Eeeeuuuwww! We looked at each other in disgust. What had we gotten ourselves into?

***

Having been raised in a small town where nearly everyone was of Scandinavian or German extraction including myself, I delighted in meeting people of so many different origins. One of my classmates was a sweet, quiet young woman who had been a pharmacist in Viet Nam. She had come to Hawaii to visit and while she was there, the Viet Nam war ended.

What a time that was. Television news stations showed US Marine helicopters loading people to quickly evacuate them out of Viet Nam while they could. People clung to the runners and doors, their feet waving in the air, and tried to climb in as the helicopters hovered over the ground attempting to take off. The news showed some local men pulling women and children out of a helicopter, as the men scrambled to get on themselves. It was horrible to watch yet I couldn't turn away. A nightmare for so many people there.

I felt bad for my classmate. She was unable to return to her husband and children in Viet Nam. The U.S. did not accept her pharmacy license so she had to retrain to support herself. It was a terrible time for her. She joined our medical technology group and we enjoyed having her as a fellow student. She was able to communicate with her family through letters. Years later, I heard she was finally able to reunite with them.

Liz worked retail in a health food store and at times was a tour guide at the Mission House Museum, one of my favorite museums. We studied together in the evenings. We each had different strengths and helped each other understand difficult concepts. Her mind grasped abstract concepts better than mine did and I was able to assist her with math problems.

We always sat up front in the classroom and taped our instructors' lectures on a used recorder. Evenings, we sat at one of our kitchen tables and poured through our notes to see what we'd missed. Studying became enjoyable as we listened to the tapes together. Amy played next to us as we studied. Sometimes we'd eat dinner as we studied. I felt secure in the knowledge that my professional life marched along on the right track. I knew I'd found my niche in life.

Besides learning theory and microscopic morphology, our class also had to learn to perform tests manually, operate and troubleshoot complicated machines, and acquire practical skills such as drawing venous blood from patients. We wouldn't learn to draw arterial blood for blood gasses until after we were actually employed as certified lab techs because of the potential nerve damage to the patient. Unlike veins, arteries are surrounded by a network of nerves.

"We're going to practice venipuncture (drawing venous blood) on each other today," my instructor said in class.

I was teamed with another student, a quiet male. Hmm, how do I do this again, I wondered. I couldn't remember how to apply the darned tourniquet. Around the arm, twist, pull one end through halfway for quick removal. Although I thought I did it exactly the same way the instructor showed us, the stupid thing fell off each time.

My hands perspired from my nervousness when I plunged the needle through the skin of another human being for the first time, searching for a vein, hoping to see the first rush of blood in the bore of the needle. Shoot! Nothing. Come on blood, where are you?

The syringe felt slippery in my hand and I tried to steady it but my hands slipped as I tried to maneuver the needle to a different spot. Still nothing. Too scared to try further and not wanting to hurt my fellow student, I pulled the needle out of his arm. I looked around. The only consolation calming my nerves was that everyone else appeared as scared and inept as I felt.

Then I role-played as the patient. My fellow student's hands shook. I tried not to notice and had to look away. I hate getting stuck with a needle. Initially it hurt but then the thought went through my head, *Hmm, this doesn't hurt now at all. It actually feels nice and warm. Weird.* Then I braved a look.

The needle had come out of my arm. No wonder it didn't hurt! I looked up at him. The quizzical look on his face told me he had no idea what had happened. He was concentrating so hard on pulling back on the syringe that he didn't see anything else. Perspiration beads dotted his forehead. He continued trying to pull the plunger back on the syringe and couldn't figure out why he was only getting air. Poor guy. The tourniquet still pinched my upper arm and my blood was oozing all over my arm onto the desktop, warm and sticky, spreading across the table.

"Uh, the needle came out," I said.

He looked and then in a panic, ripped off the tourniquet and began wiping up the mess with shaking hands.

"It's okay," I said, over and over. "Honest. You didn't hurt me."

He didn't seem comforted by my words and didn't say a word. I assumed he was so embarrassed and possibly so mortified that he couldn't even apologize. When he finished cleaning up the bloody mess, he ran out of the room.

We all improved after much practice. When I was his "patient" again, he was successful and beamed. Eventually, all of us began to gain that important skill and our self-confidence increased. It required a lot of practice but step by step, we moved closer to our goal.

***

Although I was finding my professional passion in school, I knew that being a mother was my true passion. On my days off, Amy and I would *go beach*, as the islanders say. Every now and then rain sprinkled through the sun's rays. The islanders called it liquid sunshine.

With her shock of blonde hair amidst the sea of darling dark-haired Asian and Polynesian children, Amy always stuck out at the beach. Once, for a second, I looked at her and thought—what a dunce her father was for leaving us. What he was missing! His loss. He and his parents hadn't expressed any desire to see her. She was so cute. I felt sorry for them. And then the thought quickly buried itself again, deep inside my heart into that hard-to-reach place.

While lounging on Waikiki beach watching Amy play in the warm wet sand one day, I noticed a Japanese film crew to my left. The way people acted, I concluded it was a male star filming a commercial right on the beach. He must've thought her adorable because his crew came over and talked to me. I didn't understand a word because they spoke Japanese but I discerned the star wanted Amy in his commercial. So I nodded and watched everything from the sidelines on the beach just a few feet away—a proud Mama. The whole friendly Japanese crew doted on her while filming, obviously enamored by her. Unfortunately I never got to see the commercial because it only showed in Japan.

Amy and I frequently ventured to the International Marketplace in Waikiki and ate at Ferrell's Ice Cream Parlor, even having a few birthday parties there. Linda sometimes joined us. Another year my friend Liz came along. We invited Amy's friends for dinner and ice cream, and the waiters all sang "Happy Birthday" to her. We loved their Hawaiian burgers topped with pineapple slices.

When my parents visited, Amy and I took them through that marketplace. We caught a hula dancing show on stage in the back and visited the Polynesian Cultural Center on the northern part of the island.

My parents also took the two of us to the Big Island of Hawaii where we saw black sand beaches from the volcanoes, stayed in a nice hotel, ate delicious food, played shuffleboard, swam and traveled around.

Dad took Amy and me snorkeling in Kealakekua Bay on the Big Island, some of the clearest water on this earth. Then Dad and I went scuba diving there. This was where Captain Cook, the British explorer who discovered the Hawaiian Islands, was killed in a battle against the islanders in 1779. I desperately clung to the instructor's arm as we descended fifty feet into a different world. Huge schools of big and little fish swam past, not paying any attention to us. I never let go of the instructor's arm as we glided through the clear cool water. I wanted to reach out and touch one of the larger fish but I didn't possess the nerve. My slow rhythmic breathing, in and out, provided the only sound in that underwater world.

It was an experience I'd never forget—pure peace and wonderment. My parents, a retired teacher and secretary who raised six children, weren't rich by any means so I greatly appreciated this one-time treat. It wasn't cheap. They had never been to Hawaii before and enjoyed themselves also.

***

Toward the end of the Medical Technology degree program, I interviewed and obtained a job at Children's Hospital as a lab aide. It was the mid-1970s and the hospital was an old, small building tucked away behind many large tropical trees. A barely visible sign stood on the side of the street announcing its existence.

I parked my car, an old green VW bug that thankfully never failed me, and looked once again in awe at the old structure. My first medical job. Working there would provide me with great experience in the art of phlebotomy—performing venipuncture to draw blood for lab testing. I needed the experience badly. It takes a long time to develop a high level of skill. I was nervous but soon discovered they kept me so busy, I didn't have time to think about my nerves, only the children.

One of my first patients was an eight-year-old boy who had juvenile diabetes. Each day, lab aides poked this young boy numerous times with needles for blood sugar testing and nurses poked him again to give him his insulin. Wearing my white lab coat over a brightly colored blouse, white pants and white nursing shoes, I entered his room with my venipuncture tray to draw his blood. I planned on just doing a little finger-stick on him—quick and easy.

Light brown hair topped his narrow, thin face. He huddled in a corner and watched my every move with frightened eyes.

Poor kid. I sat down on the bed and spoke softly, trying to gain his trust. "Hi. You can stay there if you want. Or you can come sit down on your bed. Whatever you want. This'll only take a second. Promise! One quick little poke on your finger. Like a fast mosquito bite. Then it's all over, in one second."

But when he saw the small lancet in my hand, he pulled his hand away. "No. I don't want my finger stuck. That hurts. Just put a

17

needle in my arm." He looked like he was about to cry.

Oh man, I felt like the bad guy in a movie. I didn't want to upset him. What he must go through on a daily basis, I couldn't imagine. Finger-sticks do hurt because of all the nerves located in the fingertips. If the phlebotomist can slip a small needle directly into a vein, there is usually less pain involved than poking fingertips with a lancet. But veins can be difficult to find on a child.

"Okay, if that's what you want." I'd have done anything to make him feel less afraid. He sat down on the bed and I stood up. Leaning over, I felt the veins in his arms. My fingers sensed thick, hard, calloused tissue instead of soft and spongy veins, sending a shot of alarm through me. He had been poked so many times that scar tissue had built up beneath his skin. I knew the scar tissue would plug any needle before it got into the vein, making it impossible to get any kind of blood sample on him.

I sat down and gently held his hand. I spoke in a calm voice, trying to comfort him. "I'm sorry, but I'm not going to be able to do it that way. It just won't work. I'm going to have to stick your finger. Just a tiny poke. Real quick, I promise."

His eyes widened in horror. "No!" He yanked his hand away and wrapped both arms around his body. He jumped up and stepped backwards, away from me, back to his safe corner.

I couldn't blame him. He was just a child, confused and scared. Sighing, I went back to the hallway to find a nurse and tell her what happened.

"I know," she said. "He absolutely refuses a finger-stick. You'll just have to find a vein."

"I can find a vein easily enough. Problem is, they're all covered with scar tissue."

She shrugged her shoulders. "You'll have to try. You can do it, I know you can."

Gee, no pressure, I thought. With resolve, I reentered his room. His face held so much pain as he looked at me. He sat back on his bed. I searched his whole body—hands, arms, feet—but the few veins I found felt thick and hard. I had to try, so I took a pediatric needle, mentally crossed my fingers, said a short prayer and plunged it straight into a vein.

Nothing.

Damn. I didn't want to keep poking him, creating even more scar tissue in his veins and worsening the situation. Sighing in defeat, I informed the nurse that the doctor would have to draw the blood because I was the only aide on duty. I had to return to the lab empty-handed—a failure. Would a more experienced phlebotomist have had better luck? I didn't know but the thought plagued me full of self-doubt. I felt horrible and looked forward to gaining more experience.

***

Before starting to work at Children's Hospital, I had not realized how pediatric patients presented the most difficult problem to draw. While working there, I experienced many young ones kicking and screaming. Someone would have to hold them down while I drew their blood. I had to chase a flailing arm while trying to hit a tiny moving target. Children's Hospital proved to be a hard place to start my career.

Occasionally I stepped into a patient's room carrying my drawing tray and a patient's relative asked, "Which window did you fly in?"

The thought, "Well, you ignorant person, I'm not a vampire, I'm a skilled professional devoting my life to helping people" ran through my mind while I remained silent. Why do people say things like that? I forced a friendly smile on my face although I was seething inside, at the same time realizing I was way too sensitive. Other phlebotomists seemed to laugh it off, but it upset me. "I just need to get a sample," I said. "I'll be done in a second."

Much later, it occurred to me the patients' families were probably nervous and scared, which explained why they acted that way. When they were rude to me, I didn't stop to think they may have been scared.

I worked four eight-hour shifts a week. Assigning me only thirty-two hours, the hospital classified me as PTNB—Part Time No Benefits. No paid vacations. No sick leave. No medical insurance. Zero. Zilch. How ironic to work in a hospital and not get medical insurance. I really felt used but I needed the job. Desperate times. At least I made enough money to scrape by but not having medical insurance made me uneasy.

For a while I worked evenings and enrolled Amy in an evening-child-care-center she enjoyed. The tug between needing to finish my courses, work to support us, and the desire to spend time with my daughter, created a war inside me. A social life would come later, but I enjoyed my time with my fellow students. They made my classes fun and we could always find a day off to *go beach*.

My scheduling lab supervisor at work, a medical technologist, approached me that first December day. "I need you to work Christmas."

"Christmas lands on my day off," I said. What a relief. I did not want to work Christmas, my favorite day of the year. I wasn't going to give up my day off to go to work on Amy's and my holiday together.

My supervisor straightened her back. She stared at me and her voice took on an air of authority. "I know, but we need you to work."

"No, sorry, I can't," I said as nicely as I could. Even though it meant time-and-a-half, spending the day alongside my daughter meant more to me than a little bit of extra money. Who wanted to send their child to a babysitter on Christmas? Certainly not me.

Her eyes glared. "Can't? Or won't?" The sharp words shot out of her prim thin lips like little bullets out of a machine gun.

The injustice of working with no benefits and being expected to cover Christmas on my day off ticked me off. I snapped back. "Won't!" I stared her straight in the eyes, daring her to argue with me. "Get me benefits and I'll work Christmas."

That was a bluff because I knew she'd never come through. She didn't have the power. But if she could've pulled it off, it would have been worth it to work on Christmas Day. I needed benefits—paid vacations to spend with Amy, paid sick leave, and medical insurance.

My supervisor stared at me in shocked disbelief.

I turned around and left, proud I'd stood up for myself, a rare occasion in my life at that time.

I didn't get benefits until months later when I graduated and the hospital hired me as a certified lab tech, forty hours a week on dayshift. I did enjoy spending Christmas Day at home with my daughter that December.

While still an aide, I walked the floors of the hospital my entire shift to draw venous blood samples and take them back to the lab for the techs to analyze. Wonderful exercise and it kept me slim. I enjoyed the interaction with patients.

Our young cancer patients broke my heart. They didn't understand what was happening to them. The fear in their eyes haunted me. Seeing these children with frail bodies, some wearing slightly crooked wigs, stirred a variety of feelings in me—sadness for them, happiness and relief that my child was healthy, and guilt over feeling any happiness at all.

Sometimes a nurse asked me a technical lab question I couldn't answer yet because I was still a student. Occasionally one scrunched up her face, looked me up and down, and said, "Well, you're lab, aren't you?"

"I'm an aide," I explained. And thank you for trying to make me feel stupid and inferior to you, I thought. I started out resenting nurses who exhibited superior attitudes. It took months for me to realize many of them were very nice. Since I didn't have much experience, I lacked a feeling of security in my professional skills. This probably caused the occasional superior attitude to bother me. Eventually I found the ability to simply ignore the intermittent rude one and laugh it off. I wanted to think of myself as part of the medical team, working alongside skilled lab techs, nurses, x-ray techs and other medical professionals for the patients' welfare. Helping people and giving meaning to my professional life.

Usually after a difficult draw, I pushed open the swinging doors to return to the lab and felt glorious relief. I rolled my shoulders, easing out the tension. I looked forward to finishing school and becoming a full-fledged certified tech, when I would stay in the lab and only occasionally have to deal with finding impossible veins, screaming and kicking patients, and haunted looks in the eyes of dying children.

Every time patients saw me, I had a needle or lancet in my hand, ready to inflict pain on them. It made me feel bad. I wanted patients to like seeing me, to think of me as someone helping them.

On the other hand, when I had a difficult patient and

succeeded in inflicting very little pain, I felt a sense of accomplishment. Part of me would miss the interaction with patients when I became a tech, sitting in the lab all day performing tests. Yet another part of me yearned to begin the academic side of medical technology. I needed that mental challenge.

When our by now small class finished taking all the required courses, we studied together for the ASCP exam—American Society of Clinical Pathology—a national exam we had to pass to qualify for certification to work as lab techs. Some students in our class couldn't make it and had dropped out along the way. The rest of us who'd made it through bought study guides and drilled each other. Studying together alleviated the stress we felt. We even had fun taking breaks, laughing, gossiping, drinking coffee, rejoicing in each other's correct answers.

Liz and I also got together and studied for that test. She worked and had a boyfriend but still found time to buckle down and study. Those sessions were the most fun and rewarding since we had helped each other down this long and difficult road, motivating each other and pushing each other to do our best.

We all passed. The students who may not have passed had previously dropped out of the program. Our entire class found jobs. As a student, Liz had trained in a hospital lab that tested samples from leprosy patients. But now as a graduate, she became a tech at a national hospital chain which had a clinic in Honolulu. Another student got a job in genetics research. Others went to various hospitals around the island. Some went to private clinics.

I switched roles from aide to tech at Children's Hospital. I attached my ASCP pin to my lab coat with pride. And new adventures began.

***

Soon after I moved up from aide to tech, Children's Hospital merged in the middle of the night with Kapiolani Hospital, Honolulu's OB/GYN hospital, named after Queen Kapiolani. A decade earlier in the sixties, a baby boy had been born there who grew up to become the President of the United States in 2008.

Ambulances transported our pediatric patients across town to Kapiolani Hospital. The merge of these two hospitals resulted in

Kapiolani Children's Medical Center--KCMC. One day I went to work at Children's Hospital and the next day I drove in the opposite direction to KCMC. Everyone exuded excitement about the merge. The feeling permeated the hallways. After the remodeling, KCMC was a beautiful hospital and the lab spread out much bigger and brighter than the one at Children's.

Even though I felt excited and happy, the increase in responsibility made me anxious. I'm not going to say "a tech and not just an aide" because lab aides are highly skilled professionals and valuable members of the lab team. But I had worked hard to get to the level of lab tech and wanted to do a good job. I was nervous but also thrilled to work at this historic institution I had read so much about.

Construction on the original Kapiolani Hospital finished long ago in 1890. Up until then, island women and their babies had a high mortality rate. As I worked at this hospital, I couldn't help but think of Queen Kapiolani and how her people had loved her. Because of my love of history, I went to the library and researched the Queen. I wanted to know why she felt driven to start a women's hospital and found interesting facts concerning her life and the period in which she lived.

I often imagined what it must have been like on the island before 1890. My imagination proved vivid and went something like this:

"A'ole. 'A'ole. Lawelawe lima ko'u kaikamahine."(No. No. Help my daughter). A man wailed with anguish. He hurled his large body on the ground. His fists pounded against the wet grass as rain beat down upon him sparing no mercy. Long gray hair hung in wet clumps around his distressed face.

Strong winds bent the palm trees, forcing their fronds to sweep the soaked ground. The vicious storm beat the Pacific's waves into froth as they crashed against the sandy shore a few feet away.

A younger man exited a hut. His black hair tumbled down his back in thick waves. His sorrowful eyes gazed at the dark sky. Rain splashed on his handsome face. His large arms reached toward the heavens and he called out, "Makua! Ko'u wahine a me keiki moe lepo. Kekahi kanaka ho'olu'olu lawelawe lima." (Father! My wife and child are dead. Someone please help.) Powerful gusts of air fought him as he pushed his way toward the older man. Bending down, he helped the rain-soaked elder to stand. "Makuahunoai kane. Hele mai loko."(Father-in-law. Come here, inside.)

Grief had drained all the older man's energy. He leaned on his son-in-law as he struggled through the gale back to the hut. Back to his dead daughter and newborn grandchild.

I imagined Hawaii's Queen Esther Kapiolani sitting in her room in Iolani Palace a few miles away as she watched the storm out her window. Her smooth black hair was pulled into a bun at the nape of her neck. Silver hoop earrings adorned her ears. A shell necklace draped gracefully over her neck. A long flowing purple dress displaying shell buttons down the front covered her generous-sized body. But these beautiful things couldn't cover the look of worry etched on her face.

A rap on the door sounded.

"Enter."

A house servant, a girl of seventeen years, tip-toed in and bowed. She wore a gold and brown muumuu that brushed the tops of her bare feet. "Ko'u Kuini."(My Queen).

"Yes, my child."

"I bear sad news, Ko'u Kuini. Another of our island women has died while giving birth."

The queen shook her head. Her shoulders slumped and she gazed out the window again. After a few moments of silence, she spoke in a soft, quivery voice. "And the child? Did the keiki live?" She held her breath, dreading the truth but needing to know.

The young girl gazed at the polished wooden floor and shook her head.

Queen Kapiolani pulled the girl toward her and wrapped her arms around her servant. Tears streamed down the queen's cheeks. Her voice a whisper, she muttered, "Too many of our island's women die while giving birth."

The queen rocked back and forth, cradling the girl like a mother holds her own child. "I must help stop the dying. They need better care. I ka wa ho'ohanau." (In their time of giving birth). A moan rose from deep within the older woman and she released her servant. "Go, my child. I must think."

In the next few days, she sought out doctors and nurses to ask them what they needed in order to help the island women.

Queen Kapiolani loved children. Her people knew her for her philanthropy. "While traveling around my kingdom, I see often it's too hard for a doctor to get to all our women if there are problems when their time has come," she told the doctors. "What can I do to help my people?"

Her medical advisors expressed the need for a central hospital for any disadvantaged Hawaiian mothers and mothers-to-be. The Queen immediately started organizing bazaars and luaus for the wealthier islanders to help raise money. She wanted to build a hospital for her kingdom's pregnant women and their babies.

In 1890, Kapiolani Maternity Hospital in Honolulu was born. Its motto proclaimed "Kulia I Ka Nuu."—Strive for the Highest. The hospital greatly improved the life expectancy of Hawaii's mothers and newborns. Queen Kapiolani also raised money for Kauikeolani Children's Hospital, finished in 1909.

After the merger of these two great hospitals in the 1970s, pregnant women, women giving birth, women experiencing gynecological problems, women suffering from cancer, victims of rape, along with newborns, premature babies, and sick children filled the floors of KCMC. That's where I proudly worked.

***

As a certified tech, I had a nice schedule at KCMC—six a.m. to two-thirty p.m.—and only worked two out of five weekends, versus two out of four weekends at most other hospitals. Loved it. Amy bussed to school at Nu'uanu Elementary School, located next to Queen Emma's Summer Palace in an area where huge trees, green lawn and flowers galore covered the ground. The Saturdays I worked, she spent at the YWCA down the street, taking classes such as dance, swimming, or arts. Sundays she went to a Polynesian neighbor's until I got home before 3:00 in the afternoon.

At the beginning of my shift in the lab, I really enjoyed the freedom of the early morning routine. We technologists helped the lab aides draw the blood samples for the morning's routine tests. The receptionist sorted the requisition slips into piles according to location in the hospital. I grabbed a stack, stocked a tray, and left the lab. It usually took approximately forty-five minutes on the floor.

I loved the early mornings. At six a.m., quiet reigned throughout the hospital as I walked the hallways. The frantic running around in the laboratory, phones ringing, doctors demanding, machines whirring, techs fulfilling orders and churning out stats, didn't begin for another hour.

One morning, however, I made my way to the basement, to L&D—Labor and Delivery. Palpable stress hung in the air, greeting me as soon as I rounded the corner. The moans of women in labor permeated the atmosphere. Nervous fathers paced up and down. Frantic looks covered the faces of the residents as they held the lives of women and babies during difficult deliveries in their inexperienced hands.

Armed with my tray of needles, tourniquets, bandages and various colored tubes indicating different anti-coagulants, I went from room to room drawing blood for morning rounds. Just as I was leaving L&D to return to the lab with the collected samples, a nurse handed me another requisition slip. "We need this stat," she said. I took the paper and entered the labor room of a lovely, heavily pregnant Polynesian.

"Is my baby going to be okay?" she asked as soon as she saw me, her face frantic from worry. Small beads of perspiration collected on her forehead. Her olive skin was flawless. Thick black hair was pulled back from her face.

What could I say? I didn't know anything about her case, and even if I did, it wasn't my place to say anything to her. "You're in good hands here. The doctors are all good," I said, trying to reassure her as I took out my vacutainer needle and tubes to draw her blood.

"There's something wrong with me. They have to take my baby out, but they don't know if it's ready yet or not."

No wonder she appeared worried. When done, I reached over and squeezed her hand gently, giving her a smile. I hated not knowing anything. I wished I could do more to help her. Relieved I had been able to collect the sample quickly and easily, I wanted to sit next to her for a while and comfort her but I had to get back to the lab. The remoteness between the patients and the lab bothered me occasionally and today was one of those times.

I hurried to the elevator. When I reached the hematology

department I called out, "Stat," then dropped off the rest of the samples throughout the various lab departments before making my way to chemistry where I was assigned to work for the rest of the day. It was almost seven a.m.

Everyone worked in a nonstop frenzy until we completed all the morning routine testing and the occasional stat. When I returned from coffee break at ten o'clock, a stat amniocentesis sample came in to the chemistry department for fetal lung maturity testing. I observed the name—it was the same Polynesian lady I had met that morning in L&D.

Evidently, the doctors needed to perform a Caesarian-section as soon as possible, for the health of the mother. They wanted to wait as long as they safely could until they knew the baby's lungs had developed enough for it to survive without developing RDS—Respiratory Distress Syndrome.

Our lab performed fetal lung maturity tests to analyze the function of the surfactants in the amniotic fluid. While the sample spun in the centrifuge, I carefully measured and made seven serial dilutions of ethanol. Surfactants are chemicals that reduce surface tension to prevent the alveoli in the lungs from collapsing. If there's enough surfactant in the amniotic fluid to overcome the anti-foaming action of the ethanol, then the lungs of the baby are mature enough to function outside the womb. RDS rarely occurred when the index read greater than forty-seven percent.

I added exactly one-half milliliter of the precious fluid, no bigger than one drop, to the first vial of forty-four percent ethanol and shook vigorously for thirty seconds. Bubbles appeared.

Repeating the same procedure, I checked at forty-five percent. Bubbles. Good.

Forty-six percent. Bubbles. Good.

I held my breath and added the amniotic fluid to the forty-seven percent tube and shook it for thirty seconds. Yes! Strong bubbles appeared at the top of the tube.

Smiling with relief for the mother, I repeated the procedure using the forty-eight percent vial. Just a few small bubbles again. This baby had fully matured lungs.

The vials at forty-nine percent and fifty percent showed no bubbles but that was okay. It took forty-nine percent ethanol to overcome the amount of surfactant in the baby's fluid—a great sign the lungs were mature and the baby could join the world and meet its Mama.

I wrote up my report by hand—we couldn't imagine the concept of computers yet—and took it to the front of the lab to be delivered to L&D immediately. I also called the results to the floor.

A half-hour later, a scared looking resident ran into the lab looking for me. He found me in chemistry, working on other tests. "Are you sure of those results?" he asked, his youthful eyes begging. "I'm going to be taking the baby out if these results are correct. I need to know. Are you sure?"

He looked so frightened. I felt sorry for him. What a lot of responsibility on all our shoulders, I thought. Merely a young resident, this baby's life depended on his decision, and the life of the mother. He desperately needed reassuring. I stared him straight in the eye and said, "Yes, the test shows those lungs are mature. There's no doubt."

He stared at me for a few seconds as if searching for the right answer. Then he took a deep breath and nodded. "Okay," he said. "If you're sure. Then I'll schedule surgery." He left.

I immediately wondered, O dear Lord, what have I done? I let out the breath I had held and grabbed the edge of the counter to steady myself. What if I was wrong? I worried the rest of the day. Later at home, I tossed and turned in my bed. What if I had made a mistake? What if I misread the results? What if my concentrations or dilutions had been off? What if they took the baby and it develops RDS and dies? I tortured myself and barely slept.

The next morning the alarm woke me at four-thirty a.m., cruelly forcing me out of bed before I had had enough rest. When I arrived in the laboratory at six a.m., I surveyed the schedule to see where my supervisor had assigned me for the day. It said NICU— Neonatal Intensive Care Unit.

I made my way down the hallway to the unit where I'd remain for the day, drawing samples on the incubator babies there for the main lab and also drawing capillary blood gasses for me to run on the blood gas machines we kept in our corner of NICU. Our lab assigned one tech to NICU per shift. We had our own area to the side with two blood gas machines, a chair, and a countertop where requisition slips lay in a pile. I enjoyed working there, interacting with different personnel and getting to know the nurses. I also enjoyed seeing the babies.

After calibrating and readying the machines for my shift, I grabbed the pile of NICU requisitions in my in-box. I donned a gown, mask and gloves then made my way to the back of the unit and searched the various incubators to find my patients.

And there she lay—a round, pink, tiny yet healthy-looking baby girl, sleeping contentedly. Full of awe, I stood and stared at my Polynesian lady's daughter. How precious she was. Lying in her incubator and looking a lot better than the other babies there. She only had one tiny IV connected to her. No multiple needles and tubes attached all over her body like the rest of the babies had.

I stood there quite a while in amazement. A nurse I didn't know came over and asked me, "Friend of yours?"

"What?" I asked, somewhat dazed. A tear threatened to escape from my eye.

"Is the mother a friend of yours?"

"Is she okay?" I needed to know right then.

"Yes, we're observing her but she is healthy. Why? Do you know her mother?"

"No," I stammered. "I drew her blood yesterday in L&D. But I'm the one who did the fetal lung maturity test that made the doctor decide to deliver her. I didn't sleep all night last night, worried, so I'm just relieved to see the baby's okay."

A surprised look crossed the nurse's face. Her eyebrows bunched together in a quizzical manner as she glanced at me, as if she couldn't figure me out. Her head cocked to one side.

I wondered why this would surprise her. Did she think lab techs possessed no heart or emotions? Like all we cared about was our machines? As if nurses were the only ones who cared about the patients? I considered myself part of the medical team and felt concern for the patients just as much as she did. Her attitude irritated me.

I drew a CBG—capillary blood gas on the baby girl and ran it through the blood gas machine. Oxygen level, carbon dioxide, and pH registered completely normal. Whew. What a great sight those numbers were. Thank God. I nearly cried with relief as I ran the results to the pediatric-resident-on-duty.

I stood staring at that baby and a thought struck me. In

29

school, we learned to do our tests using exact measurements, standardizations, quality control, precision, accuracy, trends and shifts of commercial controls, all to ensure correct results. Medical science demands accuracy.

And of course, I knew why that was all so important. I always did my very best. But incidents like this made me fully realize the human side of my testing results. The role I had in the medical team really sunk in as I stood there.

That night I fell into a deep sleep, exhausted and fulfilled. A few days later, the baby was released. Healthy mother and baby went home.

Queen Kapiolani would have been very happy.

***

Linda, my friend from Minnesota, and I would go beach when Amy was in school and I wasn't working. Throngs of people strolled along the water's edge. Refreshment stands stood between the hotels and the ocean. It was hard to imagine Waikiki in the days when Robert Louis Stevenson sat underneath a shade tree and wrote some of his stories.

They were always relaxing days. I loved to breathe in the fresh, clean scent of saltwater mingling with the smell of suntan lotion. The sound of waves rolling rhythmically onto shore almost lulled me to sleep. Peace and quiet surrounded me, broken only by the occasional laughter of a child running along the sand.

We stretched out on our towels and soaked in the sun's warm rays. We brought books, both of us being book-lovers. I rolled onto my stomach to read, allowing me a view of the mountains jutting into the vast clear sky, and dug my toes into the warm sand.

Typically it didn't take long before a good-looking guy came along and sat down beside Linda. Then another one and soon, another one. Linda had long blonde hair, a huge bright white smile, and a figure that men loved to look at. They encircled her, their backs toward me, jumping up to bring her anything she desired. She introduced each one to me and in turn, each one glanced over at me, nodded, then returned his attention to Linda.

She was dazzling in her bikini, to be sure. I couldn't blame the guys for vying for her attention but hey, I wasn't bad-looking! I was glad I had brought a book along to occupy myself while I was busy being ignored.

When Linda went into the water, the beach boys followed her. One day I debated whether I should go in also but decided to wait. I was at a good part in my book. I took a swig of my soda, propped myself on my elbows and dug back into my mystery book. In a few minutes, a guy walked over and sat down on the sand next to me.

"Hi," he said. "Mind if I sit here?"

I put my book down, removed my sunglasses and looked at him. Cute! I sat up and smiled. "Not at all."

We proceeded to talk, asking each other's names, where we were from—the usual stuff. He was friendly. I felt relaxed in his presence. I wondered if he would ask for my phone number. *Do I have a pen and piece of paper in my beach bag in case he did?* I would gladly accept a date with this guy.

After a few minutes, he looked around and then started to lean into me. *Is he going to kiss me? Right here on the beach? When we've just met?* Bewildered and wondering what to do, I looked around to see if anyone was watching. I'm quite shy that way.

His mouth came close to my ear. Tingles went up and down my spine. Then he whispered, "Do you think your friend would go out with me?"

I stared at him for a few seconds before blinking. Did I hear that correctly? I felt like Rhoda Morgenstern sitting in the shadow of Mary Richards on the Mary Tyler Moore show.

Tired of not being appreciated by men, I shrugged and then went back to reading my book, hoping he'd get the hint and leave soon. The jerk. He finally left.

Refusing to feel sorry for myself, I focused on something positive. Being Rhoda wasn't so bad. She even ended up having her own TV show. I was happy enough. I enjoyed my job. I had a future. I kept busy. I had friends. I had a healthy, adorable daughter whom I loved with all my heart. Life could have been worse. Who needs a man?

Who was I kidding?

There'll be someone special for me someday. That became my mantra. Then I returned to my book where I could immerse myself in a fictional world until that actually happened.

***

Nancy, a new tech in our lab, came from the mainland and replaced a tech in hematology who had left us. A nice lady, Nancy was in her mid-thirties and divorced. Even though she had years of experience behind her, she still had to go through two weeks of training because every lab is different with various methods, machines and record-keeping systems. After finishing a training period, she worked fulltime in hematology.

Within a month I overheard Nancy request a one-week vacation. "I want to go to New Jersey for a friend's wedding next month."

I could barely believe what I was hearing. She'll never get away with it, I thought. I scooted my chair on wheels closer to the door and held my breath to hear better.

"We're too busy and already have someone who's requested leave that week," our supervisor's voice came loud and clear.

"She's a close friend of mine. I just got notice of the wedding. I want to go." Nancy sounded determined. Pretty daring for a newcomer on staff.

"No. I can't let you go." I visualized our supervisor shaking her head. She loved to shake her head. "We'll be short staffed. We don't have the coverage. Sorry."

Silence. "And if I go anyway?" she asked.

"There won't be a job waiting for you when you get back."

Wow. Asking for vacation when you've just started a job. That takes nerve. I kind of admired her though for having the guts to do that. As a single mother, I was forced to be a kiss-ass. I couldn't afford doing anything that might jeopardize my job.

Nancy returned and I quickly made myself look busy. Nope. Didn't hear a thing.

The subject didn't come up again. Soon Nancy became a valuable member of our team and proved herself to be skilled, knowledgeable and hard working.

Four weeks went by fast and on a Monday morning, Nancy didn't show up. She had phoned the previous night evidently and

32

left a message that she would be "out for the week."

I wasn't too surprised. I had a feeling she might go but the supervisor didn't expect it. Too used to her employees obeying her I guess. Our hematology department was definitely short-staffed that whole week. I worked like a crazy woman the days I was scheduled in that department. Our supervisor worked overtime and scheduled some others to work on their days off to fill in the gap. I didn't like working overtime. I preferred to be home as a mother.

A week later, Nancy walked in. Nobody said a word. She grabbed a stack of requisition slips and went out on morning rounds. Then she returned forty-five minutes later and sat in front of our Coulter Counter and started processing the specimens. Everyone acted as if nothing had happened. Our supervisor didn't say a word to her concerning her leave of absence. Amazing.

After surviving that nightmare week in her absence, we were just glad she came back so we didn't have to go crazy working overtime or worse, short-staffed. We needed her and she was good at her job. I guess the people in power figured it would've been more trouble to advertise for a new tech, interview applicants, train someone new for two weeks and then hope the new person worked out all right.

Good for Nancy. She became my heroine role model. I needed someone like her to look up to. I'd noticed most females in a work environment tend to do as they're told—prim and proper, proud of themselves.

That's why I was happy Nancy had gone to her friend's wedding and bested the hospital. Even if it meant I had to bust my butt for a week while she attended the mainland wedding. I tend to side with the little guy against powerful establishments. They'd suck the blood out of you if you gave them a chance.

For example, it was so busy another day I didn't even have time to sigh. "Stat!" our lab aide called out continually. Chemistry tests kept coming in again and again. My stomach growled, begging for a cup of coffee and muffin. Morning break-time was long overdue.

Work swamped the entire lab. We needed more help. And what made it worse was that a chemistry tech had called in sick, leaving us down by one person on a busy day.

"Melissa's coming in," someone told me.

"What? I thought she called in sick!"

"She did. But we're so busy that Cheryl called her to ask her to come in anyway." Cheryl was our chief chemistry tech.

I shook my head. "Unbelievable." I couldn't imagine a supervisor having the nerve to call a sick employee at home and ask her to come to work.

Melissa walked through the doors twenty minutes later. Coughing. Pale. Blowing her nose. She looked terrible. Everyone gathered around her.

"Thanks for coming in," Cheryl said, a smile on her face, obviously proud of herself. "How are you?"

"I took some aspirin for my fever and it's down. I'll be okay."

As ridiculous as the situation was, I had to admit it sure was nice having a pair of extra hands. However, I made a mental note to myself: If you're ever home sick from work, DON'T ANSWER THE PHONE!!!

***

Glancing at the schedule for the day at work, I saw I was assigned once again to NICU. After donning a scrub gown, mask, and gloves, I gathered my materials and found the incubator for my first patient of the morning—the tiniest newborn I had ever seen. A new admit in the three days since I last worked in NICU. Black hair topped her narrow face. Tubes and needles covered her tiny body. A little Hawaiian baby.

Astounded, I asked the nurse, "How much does this baby weigh?"

"One and a half pounds."

Babies that small usually didn't survive. "Migosh. That's amazing." And I had to poke that miniature heel with a lancet! The thought scared me. Would I bruise her? Would I break a bone as I squeezed that tiny foot?

The nurse continued, "She's the smallest baby we've ever had survive here. Her mother died in childbirth. Her father doesn't think he can take care of the baby by himself, so he's relinquishing all parental rights to the mother's sisters. So far, her vital signs are stable. She's a fighter."

The tiny chest rose up and down rhythmically with each

breath of air forced into her, as she fought to stay in a world her mother had died bringing her into. I believed in the afterlife and the connections between souls in the two worlds. I wondered if she could sense her mother looking down at her from heaven, sending her love and strength to survive.

I felt bad for that father. His wife's death possibly overwhelmed him with grief and fear. Perhaps he was a bit resentful too, I didn't know. But I did suspect he would miss raising this strong and courageous little girl—a loss for him, for sure. It made me wonder if Amy's father ever thought about her. He didn't know what he was missing.

After slipping my arms through two sleeved holes in the incubator, I held the tiny foot in my gloved hands. The experience was surreal and I had to remind myself while I poked her heel that this was a living human being and not a doll. A few drops of blood flowed easily into the short capillary glass tube. The baby didn't even jerk. Whew.

I had just finished applying a spot pressure bandage when two large Hawaiian women walked in. I learned they were the two aunties from Molokai who had come to Oahu to adopt the baby. Their eyes radiated love for their sister's child, but also sadness.

The aunties gave the baby a melodic Hawaiian name. 'Olina Aheahe. "Joyful, softly blowing breeze." They came every day to see her.

The baby did surprisingly well. We all watched her grow, day by day, until she graduated from intensive care and moved to the regular nursery. Eventually the baby grew strong enough to go to her new home on Molokai.

From pictures I had seen, Molokai was breathtaking. Green rolling hills. Peaceful and quiet. It was the island where Father Damian devoted his life to lepers, eventually succumbing to the disease himself.

I never made it to Molokai but every time I read about it, it seemed almost magical. It was easy for me to imagine this little girl growing up on Molokai, full of joy and someday laughing and running in the ocean breeze, her curious face turned toward the vast blue sky, perhaps communing with her mother who watched her from above.

KCMC also housed the island's Rape Center. Victims on the island of Oahu, male or female, could go to this Center and be treated by specially-trained medical personnel.

We did the lab workups on the rape cases. In 1978 we took part in one of the most notorious cases ever on the island.

I followed the case in the Honolulu newspaper at the time. Over a period of weeks, the paper reported that a young lady in her twenties had moved to Honolulu from the mainland to start a new life. She found a nice apartment and a job she liked. Things fell into place for her, one of the articles stated.

Then one Sunday night at midnight, as she lay sleeping in her bed, the feeling of something cold and hard against her neck awakened her. She slowly sensed it was a gun.

A deep, raspy voice whispered, intimate against her skin, "I'm going to rape you and when I'm done, I'm going to kill you." For the next hour, he repeatedly raped her, echoing those words over and over in her ear. When he was finished, he shot her in the neck and left her for dead.

She stayed in bed, dazed, weak and frightened. Pretending to be dead, she waited to make sure he was gone. Then gathering her courage, the girl climbed out of bed, crawled on her elbows across the floor, and somehow managed to open her door and crawl to her elderly neighbor's apartment. She scratched at the foot of their door. The couple later reported they peered out the peep-hole but saw no one. Too scared to open the door, they ignored it.

The girl crawled again on her elbows down the hallway to the next door and scratched again. This time, a young man opened it and found her. He called an ambulance.

The EMTs rushed her to our hospital. The tests our lab performed for rape cases consisted of (1) examining under the microscope for sperm and (2) analysis for acid phosphatase—the enzyme found in semen. We also did various tests for the health of the patient, such as pregnancy and cultures for gonorrhea. To protect the victim, the samples were not labeled with a name, only identified by a number.

Those two above tests presented the only way authorities could know if intercourse had taken place. This pre-dated DNA testing. The courts had to do the rest.

Our technologist in hematology reported "No sperm seen" in the victim's vaginal-washing sample the doctor had collected.

My friend and co-worker in the lab, Brenda who worked in the chemistry department the day the samples came in, performed the acid phosphatase test on the victim's vaginal-washing. Brenda was a military wife in her forties, petite and pretty with short blonde hair. I remembered when Brenda first arrived at our lab. She came to the islands with her husband. A certified Medical Technologist, she hadn't worked in a lab for years because she'd been busy raising her children. Now that her children had grown and moved out, she decided to return to work and KCMC hired her for chemistry.

"Isn't it difficult to jump back in after so many years?" I had asked her.

"Very. It's nerve-wracking."

But she worked hard and never gave up and did fine. Full of positive energy, she zipped around the department, performing her duties and helping out anyone who needed it. I liked her a lot. We went to lunch-breaks together. She held a couple parties for the lab staff at her home on the base, and she always had a smile on her face.

Brenda was very reliable and professional, precise in everything she did. The result of the acid phosphatase level she performed on this rape case was very high. No sperm with a high acid phosphatase level indicated that the alleged rapist had undergone a vasectomy.

The trial created a newspaper sensation. The Honolulu Advertiser reported the man picked up for the crime worked as a professional hit-man for the island mafia. Middle-aged, he had a wife and grown children. He also had a girlfriend in her twenties who previously lived in the rape victim's apartment. She had recently broken off their relationship and moved out of her apartment because, she said, she feared him. Prosecutors speculated he wanted to send a message to his girlfriend—*See, that could have been you*—to scare her into returning to him.

Two lab techs from our lab testified at the trial. The hematology tech testified she had not seen any sperm in the specimen.

The second lab tech, my friend Brenda, also stepped onto the stand as a professional witness. I wished I could have been there to give her support. I knew she'd make a good witness. She testified she had performed the acid phosphatase test and the result had been high.

Later, Brenda told us in the lab, "He sat in court staring at me angrily the entire time I was testifying. He looked like he wanted to kill me." Her blue eyes widened as she described what happened. I hugged her. It was all I could do.

Now during the course of the trial, I feared for her. Every time I read about the trial in the paper I thought, Boy, I'm glad that wasn't me who did those tests. Scary. It was all any of us in the lab could talk about. We devoured all the news reports and shared what we learned.

The next day, prosecutors brought another witness—a doctor who testified he had performed a vasectomy on the alleged rapist. This information coincided with the lab's results so it was no surprise to the court.

The victim's family had flown to Hawaii to support her. She bravely appeared on the witness stand and according to continuing newspaper articles, with her head held up high, related what happened to her the night she was raped. She then identified the hit-man as her assailant, pointing to him as he sat in court. Things looked good for the prosecution and we were relieved. Until the stunning news: the alleged rapist had escaped.

The police couldn't find him. Oahu is a relatively small island but still had plenty of places to hide until he could find some way to escape to the mainland. Working for the mafia probably afforded him many connections.

Brenda's Air Force husband was out of the country at the time. With her children grown, Brenda lived alone until her husband returned from his assignment. She drove by herself to work every day.

The man's escape was a nightmare. What if he came after Brenda to seek revenge? I couldn't imagine what it was like for her. But at least she lived on the base. The hit-man certainly wouldn't be stupid enough to go on base to get his revenge on Brenda. Would he? The thought made me shiver. Who knew what connections he had?

"What does your husband think of all this?" I asked her.

"I didn't tell him that the man escaped. I didn't want to worry him."

Various people in the lab offered to stay with her on the base but she declined their offers. "I feel pretty safe on the base."

Nevertheless my stomach twisted. We all offered to help her in any way she needed. I couldn't stop thinking about her every night after I double-checked the locks on my door. As a single mother with a little girl, I felt especially vulnerable.

Days went by. The hit-man stayed on the loose. Police searched everywhere.

Brenda assured us that every night she checked every lock in her house, twice, before going to bed. In the mornings, she had to leave home at 5:15 to get to work by 6:00. It was still dark out as she climbed into her car. She bravely refused to let him run her life.

One evening I switched the news on while cooking dinner for Amy and me. I was thinking of Brenda when I heard the announcement, "Police catch escaped mafia hit-man." He had been hiding in a friend's house and a neighbor had phoned the police with his suspicions. I jumped up and down and shouted "Hooray!" What a relief.

With the lab results indicating the rapist had a vasectomy, the doctor testifying he had performed a vasectomy on the hit-man, the victim positively identifying him as her attacker and the hit-man's ex-girlfriend testifying he had once shown her his silencer for his gun, it seemed like an airtight case.

Until another stunning event rocked the court.

The defense attorney brought in a surprise witness. A distinguished looking doctor went to the stand and after swearing-in, testified, "I performed a reverse vasectomy on the man."

A reverse vasectomy? Then our tech should have seen sperm in that sample! But she didn't. Therefore, the man in custody couldn't have been guilty. At least, the man's attorney had a pretty good case to throw doubt into the jury's minds.

Damn. What was going on? How could this be?

The courtroom buzzed with the news. The judge then ordered a sperm count on the man. The court sent his sample to the state lab to perform. The sperm count read very low.

The prosecution called our pathologist—a doctor who is the

lab's medical supervisor—to testify. We had a wonderful pathologist. He testified, "With a sperm count that low, it would be unlikely to see any sperm. We dilute the samples with saline to maintain viability of the sperm. With the combined low sperm count, and the saline dilution, it's not surprising that the lab didn't see any sperm in the victim's vaginal-wash sample."

The newspaper reported "The courtroom breathed a sigh of relief."

After a short deliberation, the jury convicted.

Brenda worked in the lab the day we heard the news of his conviction. We surrounded her and cheered her for keeping her cool.

According to a later newspaper report, the victim moved back to the mainland. That didn't surprise me. I wouldn't have wanted to stay here either if that happened to me. Over the years I haven't forgotten that victim and pray she has recovered emotionally from her ordeal.

The closest I ever came to being raped years before couldn't compare to what that poor girl had been through. I had the nicest neighbors down the hall—a young couple with a baby. The husband was Hawaiian. He was an easy-going sweet guy and a loving father to their two-year-old boy. He once told me he had been in the Army. Some of the soldiers weren't friendly to him at first, thinking he was Hispanic. But when they discovered he was actually Hawaiian, they thought that was cool and everyone wanted to be his friend. Terrible racism.

He had a brother whom I met a couple times. I wasn't interested in him. No sparks on my side but I could tell he was interested in me.

One afternoon Amy—who was not quite four years old at the time—napped in our back bedroom. Real Estate is expensive in Hawaii and all I could afford was a small one-bedroom apartment. A knock sounded at my door. I opened it. The brother of my neighbor down the hall stood in the doorway.

A glazed look played across the features on his face. His pupils appeared very dilated. Oh, no. High on something.

Well, maybe he was just looking for his brother.

"What's up?" I stood blocking the doorway and closing the door halfway.

"I came to see my brother but they're not home. So I thought I'd stop here and say Hi." He pushed his way in and shut the door.

What the heck? Now how was I going to get rid of him. I didn't want to hurt his feelings but I just wasn't interested. And his rude behavior irritated me.

Before I could gather my thoughts, he pushed me against a wall and pressed his body against mine. Hard. He reeked of weed. He moved so fast I didn't have time to react.

His hands touched me everywhere. I tried to push him away. *Migod, this guy is solid muscle!* He didn't budge. I was only five feet three inches tall and weighed one hundred eight pounds. I was helpless against his strength.

He forced his lips on mine. Yuck. I wrenched my head back and forth as he tried to kiss me. Fear gathered in my gut and rose to my throat. My arms pushed against his chest with as much force as I could muster but I couldn't stop him. My entire body pressed against the wall behind me. I could barely grab a breath. I couldn't even kick him.

My skin retracted every place he touched me, rebelling against every touch. I wanted to scream but I didn't make a sound. I knew if I screamed, it would wake up Amy and she would walk into the living room to see her mother being raped. I didn't want her to be traumatized. Protecting her was foremost in my mind. And even if I did scream, would anyone hear me and come to help? Probably not. TVs blared from various apartments as people lived their own lives.

My only phone was in the kitchenette, just inches away from me but I couldn't reach it. I couldn't reach anything to use as a weapon. Trapped, I kept repeating, "Stop it," but I could tell he wasn't planning to stop. My mind couldn't function. My instinct made me fight but my legs were trapped. Would I even have a chance against him? I feared I wouldn't but kept trying anyway, refusing to give up. My hand pushed up against his chin but I couldn't do anything about his hands. He started to pull at my shirt.

Suddenly, he froze. His head turned, listening to something in the distance. I hadn't heard anything, but I was so panicked that all my senses were focused on trying to get away.

"My car!" he said. "It's being towed. I'm double parked." He jerked away and dashed out the door.

My heart pounding so hard that my chest hurt, I pounced and locked the door in a split second. As I leaned with my back against the wood, I heard for the first time the unmistakable sound of a car being towed away. I stood there shaking, my arms hugging my torso, trying to reassure myself that I was now safe.

"Wait," he shouted as he ran down the stairs. "That's my car!"

He must have gotten his car situation resolved quickly because in a few minutes he came back and pounded on my door. What an idiot. I didn't let him in. Finally he gave up and left.

I was fully clothed when he left but it was weeks before my skin stopped feeling repulsion every time I thought of that incident. Once again, God had taken care of me. I told my neighbor what had happened. He was furious and assured me his brother would never come near me again. And he didn't.

In spite of this, I didn't feel frightened living in Honolulu. So many friendly people lived there. The Aloha Spirit usually surrounded me. I knew my neighbors. Things can happen wherever one lives. Statistically, the crime wasn't that bad in Hawaii compared to many other states. And I loved it there. I knew I wanted to stay.

***

I was gaining experience at work and feeling more secure in my skills. When I walked through the lab's doors to start my shift, I became aware of a good feeling inside me. It was like my second home.

Working my way through the stack of hematology requisition slips as I sat in front of our Coulter Counter at work, I reached for the next tube. A newborn named Baby Kam in NICU. I diluted the pediatric sample then analyzed it for an H&H—hemoglobin and hematocrit—reading.

What? The hemoglobin—hgb— was 6.0 and the

hematocrit—hct—read 18 percent—both dangerously low readings indicating a low amount of red blood cells. This didn't worry me too much at first because a false low H&H can happen if the specimen is clotted. The red cells are caught up in the clot, giving a false low reading. Even the tiniest of clots can throw off results.

I pulled out a thin wooden stick and swirled it in the sample.

No clot. Not that I could see with the naked eye, anyway.

Uh-oh. Now I was worried. Even though an H&H does not require a microscopic slide reading, I made a slide anyway and examined it. I wanted to see what the platelets looked like. Platelet counts were done on a separate machine but I'd be able to get a good idea if a miniscule clot was present by looking at a slide.

To my surprise and horror, the newborn's red blood cells appeared abnormal—hypochromic, irregular shapes, fragments of red cells, no platelets at all, with no fibrin strands suggesting a clot. I sat for a moment almost in shock. I had studied this in school but hadn't encountered it in real life.

It was a judgment call and I was new in this field at the time but I didn't think I was wrong. Everything put together, this was a textbook slide of a patient with this condition. Disseminated Intravascular Coagulation—*DIC*–patients hemorrhaging internally so badly that every single clotting factor, including platelets, has been used up. The patient bleeds to death internally.

I was alone in the hematology department that day so I didn't have another tech to ask for a second opinion. Fortunately it was a fairly quiet day. Alarmed, I quickly called NICU and asked to talk to the resident in charge of this patient. When she came to the phone I identified myself and said, "It looks like Baby Kam might be in DIC," I said. "I suggest ordering a complete coagulation panel on him to find out for sure."

The resident must have turned away from the phone because she called out, "Hey! Lab thinks Baby Kam is in DIC!" She laughed. More laughter sounded in the background as her colleagues and the nurses joined in. "Okay. Sure," she said then hung up.

Unbelievable! What idiots. This was a teaching hospital and these were just residents. No real doctor would have reacted that way, I was sure. Most of the young residents I knew were pretty good and I admired them but I had never held much respect for this particular one. She walked around the hospital hallways barefoot, in her green scrubs, obviously thinking she was pretty cool. *Look at me. I'm a doctor.*

Furious, I wrote up my findings, documented my phone call, and turned in the report. When our pathologist got out of his meeting, I would immediately bring him the slide to review. If my suspicions were correct, this baby needed to be treated as soon as possible or would surely die within a couple days if not sooner.

In a little while, however, the resident walked into the hematology department. She was young, very tall, and barefoot of course. A humorous grin was plastered on her face. She glanced around with a haughty attitude. "Someone here says Baby Kam is in DIC."

I had to give her credit for at least taking me seriously enough to check out the situation. One point for her. "I only said it was a possibility and needs to be checked out with a full panel ordered."

"Is there anyway I can talk to a pathologist about this?" She still looked like she thought the whole thing was a joke, like I was an idiot or something, not a professional. But she was right for wanting a second opinion.

"He was in a meeting earlier but he might be back by now." I grabbed the slide. "Come with me." I led her down the hall to the pathologist's office.

For the baby's sake, I hoped my suspicion was dead wrong. Guilt filled me though, that a tiny part of me hoped I was right. After all, my professional reputation was at stake. What a horrible, selfish person I am to think that way. But at least the newborn boy had a chance of being saved because of what I had reported, if proper medical action was taken.

Thank God our pathologist, the chief M.D. in charge of our lab, sat in his office. I introduced him to the resident standing behind me. Our pathologist, a man whom I admired greatly, slipped the slide under his microscope and peered through the lens. He was one of the smartest doctors I had ever met and was very caring, also. After a few moments he said, "Yes, it looks like DIC."

The color immediately drained from the resident's face and alarm filled her eyes. The smile wiped right off her face in a flash. No more amused look. No more haughtiness. Muttering 'Thank you' to the doctor, she turned and practically ran down the hall.

Soon an order for a panel of stat coagulation tests came in for Baby Kam and also a crossmatch for a blood transfusion. The coagulation tests confirmed that the baby was in DIC. The mad rush to save his life began.

I felt no satisfaction at all in learning that I was right. Only relief that my education and training had helped save a patient's life, and professional pride that I had recognized the condition and stuck my neck out to tell the resident what I thought. The alarm in that resident's face and the quick action she took were enough vindication for me. If that resident learned a lesson from this situation, she might actually make a half-way decent doctor someday, I thought.

The next time the lab assigned me to NICU, I went over to see Baby Kam. There he slept, multiple monitors hooked up to his entire body. He had received a blood transfusion and was on his way to recovery. He slept peacefully, his body busy with growing and getting healthier by the minute.

Baby Kam had made it. That's what filled me with satisfaction.

There are a few patients I will never forget. Besides Baby Kam, another patient who sticks in my memory was a woman who had just given birth to a healthy baby. I ran the new mother's hemoglobin—hgb-- and it was 10.0. Normal for a female is at least 11.0 and higher but it wasn't unusual for the hgb value of a new mother to drop after childbirth due to the loss of blood involved.

Her next hgb reading later in the morning had dropped to 9. This was not a good sign.

Another sample came into the lab a little later. I ran it and her hgb this time was 8. Dear Lord! It was obvious she was bleeding out. Funny, but her doctor hadn't ordered a cross-match to be done, in case she needed a transfusion. What was going on?

Later in my shift, her hgb dropped to 7. The doctors had ordered a coagulation panel to see if her blood was clotting correctly. Her platelets were almost all gone and the other coagulation results were all abnormal. Probable DIC. But still no Type and Crossmatch panel had been ordered.

The next hgb test dropped to 6. When Labor and Delivery called later to have another sample drawn, the lab aide was busy elsewhere so I volunteered to go down to get it. I was caught up on all my work and besides, I was curious to find out the woman's story.

A crowd of people gathered in the woman's room. Various doctors, specialists, nurses and interns milled around the small area, looking at her chart and consulting each other. Just seeing all those doctors there gave me confidence that she was in good hands. The intelligence these experienced specialists possessed amazed me.

A man sat by her bedside holding her hand, his head bowed in prayer.

I learned the woman was a Jehovah's Witness. She was refusing to have a blood transfusion. A handful of elderly men dressed in suits stood outside the door, praying with sorrowful expressions on their faces.

The resident handed me a syringe of a small amount of blood from her central line and I transferred it to a pediatric purple tube. I rushed back upstairs to the lab and holding my breath, prepared the sample for a hgb reading. We couldn't automatically load pediatric samples into the machine. We had to manually dilute them first. After an eternity, numbers in bright red appeared on the screen: 5.2.

My God! With shaking hands, I dialed Labor & Delivery and reported the result. An order for a Type and Crossmatch for a transfusion had finally come in. However, the blood was sitting in blood bank's refrigerator all ready to be given to the patient but so far no one had picked it up.

I certainly have respect for people's religious beliefs and try not to be judgmental but it was eerie watching this woman slip closer and closer to death while knowing she could be saved. Her baby was perfectly healthy. Her first child. I was caught up in this case and the next time they ordered a hgb, I told our lab aide I would go down and get it.

A nurse there told me, "The hospital's lawyers are involved, trying to force a transfusion."

A look of deep sorrow and fear covered the husband's face. Tears rolled down his cheeks. His wife lay on the hospital bed with an oxygen mask covering her face, her skin pale, her thin body motionless. She looked young and pretty. Dark hair fell in moist curls around her face. I hoped those lawyers could do something for her.

Once again, the resident handed me a small syringe of her blood. It looked pale and watery as I transferred the small amount into a purple pediatric tube. I hurried back upstairs and ran the hemoglobin. This patient's sample took priority over all the others waiting on my counter by now. 4.3! Incredibly low. She would surely be dead by the next day if her doctors couldn't stop this.

She needed red cells to carry oxygen throughout her body. She needed plasma with its coagulation factors to stop the bleeding. She also needed platelets. She needed these fast. But she wouldn't take them.

Her husband could have approved a transfusion for her at that point, I was told, but he held to his wife's wishes. With grief-stricken looks on their faces, friends, family and church officials all gathered in L&D, praying for this new mother. Personally, I believe God works through doctors, nurses, and other medical professionals but legally the hospital had to respect the patient's beliefs.

Her next hgb read 3.5. Unreal. Just looking at that number gave me the chills. She was slipping away fast. I went back down to L&D to save time in case they needed more lab drawn.

Finally, a phone call came into the nurse's station. "The hospital's lawyers got a judge's order," she yelled. "We can transfuse. Let's go!"

Immediately everyone started to move. Fast action replaced standing around waiting. The husband dropped his head onto his wife's hands, muttering a prayer. He looked relieved now that a judge had taken the decision out of his hands.

I ran back upstairs to the lab to catch up on my work.

Our DIC patient received the transfusion, just in time. After receiving the blood, platelets, coagulation factors, and days of good medical care, she eventually improved and went home to raise her new baby.

Our pathologist said, "Sometimes when blood transfusions are ordered against patients' religious beliefs, patients become so depressed that they kill themselves." I couldn't imagine that happening in this case. I hoped the joy of raising a healthy baby would overcome any fears she might have had. As a mother myself, who'd had a difficult delivery resulting in bleeding,

47

infection, and three hospital roommates in succession due to my eight day hospital stay, I could still imagine the fun she would eventually have with her child, making everything all worthwhile. Babies are worth it!

***

I casually dated various men over the years I lived in Hawaii. I tended to be conservative in my relationships, waiting a long time before I got emotionally involved with anyone. Only one man in Hawaii was important enough in my life to mention here.

A mutual friend invited a man named Jack and me to her apartment for dinner—a set-up. When he first looked at me, his warm brown eyes made me feel like my body was melting into a pool of liquid butter right then and there. Tall and thin, he leaned down close to me to catch every word I said, as if my words were important to him. When he smiled, it was like he found joy in the world around him. I knew right away he was interested. And so was I.

Seven years older than I was, he previously worked in Malaysia in the Peace Corps. He had a young soul, making our age difference irrelevant. When we met, he worked for the state helping people on welfare start gardens to grow their own food.

The next day he called and asked if I wanted to go to the beach. We sat on the sand and talked and talked. Conversation with him came easily. One of the first things he said to me was, "I had cancer. Hodgkin's Disease. But I've been in remission for a long time."

Wow. I was shocked. He looked so healthy. He continued, "I have frequent check-ups and no sign of it. I feel great."

I appreciated him telling me this. It must have been difficult. He left the decision in my hands. Even knowing his history of cancer, I wanted to continue seeing him. It was in the past, years ago. He was in remission. I looked to the future.

I felt comfortable with him. The two of us eventually became good friends. He got along great with my daughter. At the age of six, Amy took to him right away, responding to his gentle and caring manner.

Once while walking along the beach by the Kahala Hilton

Hotel, Jack, Amy and I saw Michael Landon sunning himself. The star of Bonanza—and later Little House on the Prairie and Highway to Heaven—was so handsome as a young man in nothing but swim trunks, I couldn't help but stare. Thick dark hair, brilliant smile, golden-colored smooth muscular chest, flat stomach. Practically like a Greek god. Wow. He was unbelievably good-looking.

I stood up straighter and strolled past the star in my bikini. He must have seen me staring because he finally nodded, smiled and said, "Hello," then turned back to his gorgeous blonde wife in her shapely pink bathing suit. A memorable moment in my life.

After we passed him, Jack leaned over and whispered in my ear, "You can let out your stomach now."

Ha Ha. Funny. He knew me too well by then. I laughed and slipped my arm through his. But my abs stayed pulled in.

Many times I observed the warmth and friendliness of not only the local people, but also Asian tourists. They loved Hawaii. Jack and I frequently took Amy to dinner at a Chinese restaurant. He taught her how to use chopsticks. Asians frequently got a big kick out of seeing her, at the age of seven, eating proficiently with chopsticks. So cute!

We were like a little family, the three of us, the first time I experienced that feeling and I liked it. For the first time, it wasn't just Amy and me. Now it was Jack and me, teaming together to teach Amy about life's joys. He was nuts about Amy.

Jack avoided tourist places but I liked them. One of my favorite places to take Amy was the International Marketplace along Kalakaua Avenue in Waikiki. I loved to hang out there and spend entire afternoons strolling around, watching Polynesian women make tapa tapestries, window shopping, occasionally purchasing a dress, and surveying the various souvenirs. Walking around that place transported me, making me forget for a while about life's responsibilities. It was always a fun day. I bought a salad bowl made of Koa wood and a kokua nut necklace to send to my mother, and a carved model of an outrigger canoe for my Dad. I missed my family but I loved living in Hawaii.

In the summertime, my oldest sister—who was a schoolteacher—and her two daughters came to Hawaii to visit. My parents generously paid for my sister, my two nieces, Amy and me to fly to Maui from Oahu. Jack drove us to the airport to fly to Maui. What a gorgeous island. So green, it looked like a carpet had been laid over the mountains and land. We drove to the Seven Pools, passing waterfall after waterfall.

We were eating dinner in a restaurant on Maui, looking out the large glass windows to the breathtaking ocean view. Then the people at the next table said to us, "Did you hear Elvis just died?" Other patrons chimed in. Pretty soon the entire restaurant was talking about it. What an upsetting shocker for my sister and me. We were both big fans of his. It was the end of a musical era.

The next time my parents visited, we went to Iolani Palace, the only palace in the U.S. It fascinated me to walk around where Hawaiian monarchy once lived before U.S. troops took control of the Palace.

As a lover of history, I enjoyed museums. We also visited the Bishop Museum, full of Pacific Island artifacts, and the Missionary House Museum where the missionaries had lived.

We went to Pearl Harbor where the USS Arizona sank. The Memorial is beautiful. It was emotional thinking about the dead bodies buried below us.

And it was emotional each time my family returned to Minnesota. But I still loved Hawaii and wanted to stay.

***

Later that year, in the winter, I realized that the biggest drawback of working in a hospital was the holiday situation. I hated alternating Christmas with Thanksgiving. If I worked Christmas, I got Thanksgiving off and vice versa.

One Christmas Day at three o'clock I came home from work, anxious to spend the rest of the day with Amy eating dinner and opening presents but I couldn't find a parking spot. The parking situation in Honolulu was horrendous. No parking garages anywhere nearby. I drove my old Volkswagen bug around the block, around the neighborhood, up one street and down another, for more than half an hour. Couldn't find a vacant spot. Then I drove far away, willing to walk the distance if I could only find a spot, but nothing. I couldn't believe it.

What a waste of the little holiday time I had. The day slipped away. It was now late afternoon and I'm sure my babysitter was wondering where I was. So out of desperation and also exasperation, I parked too close to a fire hydrant. I knew what would happen but what else could I do? Drive around until the next morning?

Sure enough, I got a ticket and the city towed my car away. But at least I got to have some time at home on Christmas Day. I dealt with my car later.

***

A co-worker in the lab, Gloria, and I socialized outside of work. About my age, she was cute and sweet, and also an excellent lab tech. We were both single. The two of us went to lunch together on our days off, went shopping, and talked for hours. One day she told me, "My husband died when I was twenty-three. He had pneumonia but was misdiagnosed."

Words of comfort don't come easily for me sometimes. "Oh Gloria, I'm sorry. That's awful." I didn't know what else to say. Situations like this made me feel inadequate as a friend. I wanted to help but didn't know what to do or say.

Wanting to start over and get away after her husband died, Gloria eventually left the mainland, moved to Hawaii and got a job at KCMC in the lab as a technologist. One day she had news for me. "I met a guy in the Navy and he asked me out."

Yeah! Exciting.

Soon, Gloria spent all her free time with him and I only saw her at work. Her Navy man made her very happy. She and I tried to go to lunch at the same time at work so we could eat together in the cafeteria and catch up on each other's news.

He eventually proposed to her. Jack and I attended their wedding. The sun spilled its warmth over the ceremony. The scent of beautiful Hawaiian flowers wafted throughout the air at the outdoor gathering. Lush greenery surrounded us as we walked hand in hand to a decorated gazebo for the reception.

Gloria's husband was handsome with a friendly smile. Lots of tall, well-groomed Navy men in their white uniforms milled around, looking sharp and strong. They slapped the groom on the back, congratulating him. Champagne corks popped. Bubbly liquid spilled over onto the ground. Everyone raised their glasses and toasted the newlyweds. I was happy for Gloria that she had also found someone special in her life.

A few months after the wedding, the garbage workers and state custodians on Oahu went on strike. The stench of garbage hit me in the face every time I stepped outside. You'd think the wind would have carried the smell away over the ocean but it didn't. The odor hovered everywhere, disgusting everyone. Schools closed for health reasons. Amy was in third grade at the time. Her school, located next to Queen Emma's Summer Palace, threatened to close because of the strike. In order to keep the school open, a group of parents volunteered to clean. I joined the committee.

On certain days after finishing work, I met other parents at the school to empty the garbage, vacuum and clean the classrooms and bathrooms. Fathers with trucks loaded up the garbage sacks and towed them miles away to the dump. With everyone's cooperation, we managed to keep the school open.

One Wednesday, Gloria asked me, "Can you drive me home after work today?" She lived on the Naval base. Joy at being married gushed out of her. Her husband seemed nice, although I'd only met him a couple times. "My car isn't working. I got a ride this morning into town but I need a ride home."

"Oh, I wish I could, but it's my afternoon to clean some rooms at the school because of the garbage strike," I said. "How about tomorrow? I'm not scheduled for school clean-up then."

"Okay. Thanks. Maybe you could come in after work tomorrow. I'll make tea and we can visit."

I had always wanted to see her place. "Great. Tomorrow. We'll leave here, pick up Amy, drive you to the base and visit."

"Thanks. Maybe you could stay for dinner, too."

"I'd love that." How fun. I looked forward to it.

Another lab tech drove Gloria home that Wednesday, dropped her off at the front door and drove off right away, having to get home to her own husband and meal preparations.

Gloria unlocked her front door, entered her living room, and found her husband dead in the middle of the floor from a self-inflicted gunshot wound.

The whole lab heard about it the next day. We all walked around in a fog, numb with shock. I was working in the chemistry department when I heard. I thought, *I wished I had been there with Gloria so she wouldn't have been alone.*

My second and stronger thought immediately followed. If it hadn't been for that garbage strike, Amy would've been there to see that. I shuddered. That would have been horrible. Thank you, God, for that garbage strike. God was protecting Amy. He always did. What a great Father He was!

Then a doctor hurried in, looked around, recognized me, and came over to me with a paper in his hand. "I have some results here from the lab but they don't make sense. I'm sure they're wrong."

I shrugged my shoulders. I didn't know who had performed those particular tests but I lowered my voice. "There are going to be a lot of mistakes coming out of the lab today. The husband of one of our techs killed himself yesterday."

The doctor looked irritated. "Well, who can I complain to about these results?"

I gave him a sad look and shook my head. "You can complain all you want, but I guarantee you, nothing will be done about it. We're all walking around in shock."

For a moment he looked like he was going to argue. He opened his mouth to say something but nothing came out. He studied my expression for a moment. Then a look of understanding crossed his face. He closed his mouth, nodded and turned away.

News of the tragedy spread throughout the hospital. Everyone eventually learned not to harass the lab staff that day and leave us alone to grieve while we recovered from our emotional trauma.

The funeral was surreal—widowed twice by the time she turned twenty-seven. No one had any explanation as to "why." There had been no signs. It came as a complete surprise to all his friends, his Navy buddies said. We never learned details. But I didn't care about details. All I cared about was Gloria's state of mind.

After the service, I stayed for a while. Gloria sat in a chair staring into space. Her sister and I talked for a while—small talk. Gloria didn't say a word. Her parents and sister from the mainland were staying with her so I knew she had support. I gave her a hug then left.

She never came back to work. She packed her things, moved back to the mainland and stayed with her parents before beginning a new life. We kept in touch for a while. She eventually remarried and then I didn't hear from her again. The whole tragic episode saddened me. I missed my friend and hoped she ended up having a happy life.

The lab went back to its usual routine and things quickly settled down. New babies were born. More lives were saved. For so many people the beautiful islands are Paradise. But life and death happen, no matter where you live.

***

Carrying a phlebotomy tray on my early morning rounds, I walked into a room in the island's Rape Center. Because the Rape Center was located in our hospital, we saw almost every rape that occurred on the island, making it seem like there were a lot of rapes there. Actually, Hawaii's crime rate was lower than most states on the mainland.

A nurse sat in a chair, cradling a three-year-old little girl. The nurse rocked back and forth, almost hysterical.

Bumps and bruises spread over the toddler's round face. One of her eyes was so black and swollen, she couldn't see out of it. She looked like a boxer who had just lost the worst fight of her life. Her lip was swollen and cut. Bandages dotted up and down her arms.

"The mother's ex-boyfriend beat and raped her," the nurse whispered to me. "He also burned her with a cigarette. That's what those bandages are covering."

There I stood holding a needle in my hand, having to inflict more pain on this child. Please God, is there an easier way? The thought of sticking this precious child with a needle made me nauseous. "I have to draw her blood for a CBC and platelet count," I explained to the nurse.

The nurse looked at me with wild eyes on the verge of tears. She hugged the child closer to her in a protective manner. At first I didn't think she was going to let me do my job but she finally relented. "Okay, but don't you dare miss. You only get one try," she hissed and shot me a defiant, angry look.

Yes. I woke up this morning rubbing my hands together with glee and thought, Hmmm. Now what little child can I hurt today?

My heart was breaking for this child just as much as the nurse's was.

Stroking the child's back and curly brown hair, the nurse spoke to the little girl in a frantic voice. "You must be brave, sweetie. I'm right here with you. This lady just has to give you a little prick in your arm, but it will only take a second. I promise."

Gee, no pressure.

Pediatric patients are not the easiest patients in the world to draw in the first place. Their veins are tiny and hard to hit. Plus children usually are not cooperative. I understood this nurse's feelings and could see why she was upset—the entire situation was absolutely horrendous—but she wasn't helping this girl much by acting so agitated. Nursing was a tough job but so was mine.

I patted the little girl's hand and gently squeezed it. "I'm sorry, honey. You're so brave and I'm proud of you." I opened a small butterfly needle and mentally said a prayer. I always prayed before I went to work that I would do my best, but this warranted an extra prayer.

My hands shook a little from my heart pounding rapidly. I can't do this! The three-year-old held out her arm. Burying her head into the nurse's neck, she didn't move—one of the bravest patients I've ever known. My shaking fingers palpated the chubby little arm and located a tiny thread of a vein deep below the layers of baby fat. "Tiny little mosquito bite, sweetie," I said.

"Okay," she said, her voice deep and gruff, not like a three-year-old's typical voice. Holding my breath, I plunged the needle in. I would have wanted to chop off my own arm rather than to miss that tiny vein.

What struck me the most about this child was her toughness. She didn't cry. She just seemed to accept what was happening, as if this were a normal life.

Thank God I hit the vein right away and the blood sample came smoothly and quickly. When finished, I immediately packed up my things to leave, wanting the patient to forget about me as soon as she could. Anger, shock, nervousness, and heartache all combined to squeeze and twist my stomach into a knot as I left to return to the lab for the rest of the day.

When the little girl got better, she went home. I assume authorities caught the guy since they knew who he was. That frustrated me. Unless it made the papers, I usually didn't know the follow-up results of my patients and their lives. I wanted to be more involved with them and feel more helpful. I had to remind myself that doing the best I could do in the laboratory was helping these patients. They needed accurate and precise lab results so the doctors could treat them correctly.

While on early rounds a different morning, I walked into a patient's room on one of the floors. Eighty-seven years old. She lay in bed, her whole body shaking. Bruises covered her face and arms. A man had attacked and raped her. Someone found her lying on a park bench, in shock.

I froze, watching her in disbelief. The disgusting things mankind does to one another. I spoke softly to her, explaining that I had to draw some blood for some lab tests. She didn't respond, just stared straight ahead. Gently, I pulled her arm down and searched for a vein. She continued to shake but didn't resist.

She didn't look at me. She didn't say anything. I reached out and patted her hand. I didn't know what to say. It's going to be all right? This won't hurt? Everything seemed inane.

As quickly as possible, I drew her blood. I wanted to do something nice for her. I wanted to sit with her and hold her hand and talk in a soothing voice to her—to help make things better for her. I thought of my Grandma. That could've been her, lying there alone with no one to comfort her. But I had other patients and lots of work to do. I had to go.

When I left her room, I noticed her body was still shaking. I wondered about her family. Had anyone come to see her? I didn't know. Sometimes I wished I had become a nurse instead of a lab tech, so I could be more involved in patients' lives and care. I never learned if the police caught the monster who did that to her.

From six-month-old babies to eighty-seven-year-old women, we had rape cases of all ages. It's disgusting to say the least, to think that women will never be completely free of the possibility of being raped until they are laid in the ground.

***

Of all the many rape cases I worked on in the lab over the years, the courts only called me as a professional witness once.

I waited in the hallway of the chilly court building on a hard wooden bench, twiddling my thumbs. My palms got a little moist and my stomach felt fluttery. Only one person walked the hall. Her shoes clicked along the tile, echoing in the stillness.

Before I came to the courthouse, I had reviewed my lab report and was familiar with the results from months before. The only procedure I did on this case was to examine the vaginal washing for sperm.

To calm my nerves, I imagined a large courtroom full of people, the judge pounding his gavel to quiet the crowd as I walked to the front and took the stand. Then of course I would impress everyone with my professional knowledge. Just like on Perry Mason.

Instead, after the bailiff summoned me from my bench, I entered a tiny room that only had a small round table and a few chairs. Thin blue carpet covered the floor. A large window allowed a view of palm trees and blue skies. The judge in his black robe, two attorneys, a nice-looking guy with dark hair in his early twenties, and a slim, pretty blonde woman also in her early twenties, sat waiting for me. I immediately sensed the seriousness of the situation. A hot charge of intense emotion swirled around me in the cramped area, choking out the air. Anger emanated from the girl and the boy looked confused and scared. Nobody said a word.

With my right hand on the Bible, I raised my other hand and swore to tell the whole truth and nothing but the truth. The bailiff seated me at the round table. Then I stated my name, occupation, degree, certification and place of employment.

All of a sudden, I felt intimidated. What if my nerves took control of me and I blathered like an idiot? What if the prosecutor's entire case had to be thrown out because I was such a terrible witness? Quiet pervaded the small space. Everyone stared at me. I forced myself not to wring my hands or bite my nails.

"Please tell the court what you found." The judge's voice sounded calm and authoritative.

I cleared my throat and compelled my voice not to shake. I stated the number on the sample which corresponded to the defendant and the date of the test. "I did see sperm in the sample, non-motile."

"What does 'non-motile' mean?" the judge asked.

This surprised me. Isn't that a common word? "It refers to movement. The sperm were not moving."

"Can this indicate how long, prior to that, intercourse took place?" the judge asked.

Uh-oh! I hadn't expected that question. The time intercourse took place must have been crucial to the defense's case. Sometimes the sperm are zooming around, but I had reported 'non-motile.' Did this mean quite some time had passed since the incident occurred?

The boy looked scared and bewildered. He could've been any nice boy in one's neighborhood. The girl seethed with what seemed to be indignation and kept shooting the boy dirty looks. Her hands and legs kept jiggling as if she could barely force herself to sit still.

I remembered once seeing a different girl in the rape center smiling and laughing as she gave the police officer details. Her mother sat crying in a corner, upset about her teenaged daughter's alleged rape. The daughter seemed to think it was a funny joke.

But this girl in the courtroom was not laughing. She was obviously upset.

"No, there's no way to determine time," I answered.

"Are sperm usually motile in rape cases?" the judge asked.

I weighed my words carefully. "Sometimes. But the sample has been taken out of its natural environment and then we dilute it with saline. The difference in temperature and the dilution can have any effect on the sample. You just never know."

Was I babbling? Had I made any sense? When I get nervous, I have a hard time focusing. I glanced around at the people in the room. Nobody looked at me like I came from outer space, so I guess my words must have come out coherent. The judge nodded solemnly.

I was dismissed. That was it. My big court case.

When I returned to the lab the next day, everyone gathered around me, asking what happened.

I explained what I had said. "We can't determine how long it's been, can we?" I asked them, needing reassurance. What if there really was a way and I just didn't know it? I could have thrown the whole case with my ignorance. I should have stated, *Not that I know of,* instead of *No.*

But everyone shook their heads. "No, you can't. All we can

do is tell if intercourse took place. Yes or no. The rest is up to the courts."

Relieved, I realized I needed to start trusting my knowledge and experience.

That court case made me think again of the time my neighbor's brother came into my apartment. It was as if it never entered his head that I didn't want him.

I wondered if the word, "No," doesn't register in some males' minds. Perhaps from their points of view, the female really means "Yes." Maybe to this guy in court, he was doing what she wanted—just being a man. That would explain the confused look on his face. Males don't have to deal with the potential outcome of intercourse.

But to the female, "No" means "No." That young woman must not have wanted intercourse. That would explain the anger emanating from her that day in court. Two people not on the same page of thought. It wouldn't be for many years that a "No Means No" campaign began in the U.S. to educate males on this issue. Too late for this young man.

I never heard the outcome of the judge's decision. I never learned what happened to that guy. Glad I wasn't a judge who had to decide that young man's future, I only hoped I helped justice triumph for both of those young people.

***

A big part of working in the hematology department of the lab involved examining and evaluating patients' microscopic slides. Three microscopes lined up along the countertop for techs to use. On a busy, well-staffed day, two of us would sit at the microscopes working, while a third would work at the Coulter Counter machine performing cell counts.

Our hematology supervisor, Ron, stepped out for a few minutes to get some supplies. He was in med school to be a doctor and was engaged to a Blood Bank lab tech named Cathy. I liked them both.

We always had a radio on to enliven the atmosphere. At Christmastime we listened to holiday music for a month. The rest of the year, we had on a rock station. We worked together in perfect unison, everyone pitching in to finish the work. The nice thing about working at the microscope was that we could carry on a conversation. I liked everyone in that lab. Camaraderie developed between us. It felt great to be part of a professional team—all of whom I greatly admired—and to be accepted as a professional equal to them.

The harmonious voices of the Everly Brothers emanated from our radio. I loved them. I started singing with them, in a fairly loud voice, "Here he comes, that's Cathy's Clown."

Just then, Ron walked in. He froze and shot me a dirty look.

What the heck? Why was he angry? What did I do?

He continued staring at me.

Then it hit me. "Cathy's Clown." I felt horrible. "No, no, Ron. It's the song." I pointed to the radio. "The Everly Brothers. Just a song."

He relaxed and smiled. Whew. He was a nice guy and I didn't want him to think I was making fun of him because that had never entered my mind.

I only had to work two out of five weekends. On those days, Amy went to the YMCA close to our place. I signed her up for a full day's worth of classes—tap dancing, swimming, art, etc. I sent a little lunch with her.

On my weekends off, we always went to the beach, usually Waikiki but sometimes we'd try other beaches such as Ala Moana, Kahala Hilton Resort where once I had a birthday party for her and visited their Atlantic Bottlenose dolphins in the resort's natural lagoon, or way up to the North Shore where Sea Life Park was located.

One Saturday, a couple girlfriends of mine decided we should explore a beach we'd never been to. My two friends, Amy, and I drove north out of town. Someone said, "Look, up ahead, a bunch of cars in that pull-out area. There must be an accessible beach there."

I veered my old green VW to the side of the road and parked. We all got out and stood on a cliff, looking at the blue sparkling water in the distance. We found a path amidst thick foliage that looked like it led to the beach far below. "Let's try it," we decided.

We gathered our beach bags full of towels, suntan lotion, books to read, and water bottles, and began our trek down the rocky dirt path. Tree branches shaded the sunlight. Cool air greeted us as we picked our way slowly down the winding path, around bushes and palm trees. The scent of salty sea air beckoned us.

I hiked behind Amy as we followed my two friends. I happened to glance to my right. There amidst many trees, stood a Polynesian male, probably in his twenties, with his bronzed skin, muscular arms, and smooth chest. Very good-looking. He didn't notice me. Then I saw he was holding his swim trunks in one hand while pleasuring himself with the other.

Holy cow. I hoped Amy hadn't seen that. My two friends kept walking and talking, their conversation uninterrupted, apparently not seeing anything unusual. The rocky dirt path forced us to focus on where we walked. I pointed to my left, "Oh, look to the left, you can see the ocean through those trees," wanting to direct their attention in the opposite direction.

We kept hiking and soon we were well past the naked young man in the woods. Whew. That was lucky. No one saw him evidently except me. That was not something I wanted my daughter to see. I didn't mention it to my companions.

I figured the guy must've gotten turned on by all the girls in bikinis that probably adorned the beach at the bottom of our trail.

Finally we cleared the wooded area and reached sand. A soft breeze ruffled my hair and warmed my skin. We found a place to spread our towels and settled down by the water. It was beautiful. A few people but not crowded like at Waikiki Beach—perfect. Some good-looking guys we may perhaps meet?

After a while, one of my friends said, "Do any of you notice anything strange?"

I looked around. "No, why? Do you?"

She said, "Everyone here is male."

I looked down the stretch of beach and saw a bunch of guys strolling along. I turned my head and looked the other way. Another bunch of guys strolled on the sands. Some held hands. Not a single female. Except for our little group.

Oh, no! We had unwittingly invaded a gay beach! I was sure none of the men there were too happy about us being there. Nobody owned any of the beaches on Oahu. There were no private beaches. The land was all leased, so we had a right to be there. But I felt uncomfortable for invading their privacy. And I hoped there wouldn't be a repeat of the exhibition I saw on our way down the cliff. "Should we leave? This is embarrassing."

We decided it was too long of a walk to get down here. "We might as well stay." So we all jumped into the water and enjoyed the day, keeping to ourselves. We had quite a story to tell when we returned to work on Monday but we made sure never to return to that beautiful beach again.

***

A pediatric specialist had scheduled a bone marrow aspiration/study on a child. I was assigned to hematology that day, so I got the honors to assist him. Although I'd been trained on the procedure and knew what to do, I'd never done it before on an actual patient. Talk about nervous.

Wearing my white lab coat and hoping I looked professional, I arranged my needed items on a tray in the patient's room. The boy was about eight years old. It was my job to examine the aspiration, tell the doctor if he got bone marrow or not and if he did, make numerous slides for our pathologist to study for abnormal cells, then return to the lab and stain the slides.

The doctor/nurse team gave the boy a sedative through his IV, while I stood to the side waiting. They asked the boy to start counting backwards. "Ten, nine, eight" he recited, then his words began to slow down and slur as he continued counting. He didn't reach zero before he drifted off.

The nurse had already prepped the site with betadine. Wearing sterile gloves, the doctor twisted a hollow needle into the boy's hipbone. It was at that moment when I began to feel a little lightheaded. The room began to spin around me just a little bit. There wasn't much space in which to move. Four windowless walls suddenly seemed awfully close.

Is it especially warm in here? Stop it. Shake it off. You can do this. The room is not spinning. Everything is just fine. Hang in there.

Twisting and screwing the needle deeper, the doctor finally stopped. He attached a syringe and pulled back, hard, on it. Bloody fluid entered the syringe.

Fascinated, I began to gather my wits. Now that the twisting was over, my head cleared. Blood I was used to. *Whew, I feel fine now.* Wow, this is interesting.

The doctor handed me the syringe and I started to make slides.

"Did I get bone marrow?" the doctor asked.

The answer to this question was vital. If I said "yes" and then our pathologist looked at the slides and didn't find any bone marrow, the entire procedure from beginning to end would have to be repeated.

I searched the slides for visible signs of bone marrow—minute white specks mixed in with the blood. Yes, they were there. "Yes, you got it."

"Are you sure?" he persisted. "It didn't feel like I did. And I didn't see anything."

I looked again. He had done this many times, I assumed, and I knew this was my first time. But yes, it looked to me like there were white specks of marrow particles in the sample. I had to work quickly before the blood clotted. If that happened, I wouldn't be able to get the sample out of the syringe or make any more slides. The procedure required many slides. "Yes, I'm sure."

"Okay, if you say so." He removed the large pin from the boy's bone, dropped it onto his tray with a clink and removed his gloves. The nurse cleaned up the area.

I made multiple slides. Preparing a bone marrow slide is a completely different technique from making slides out of venous blood. A bone marrow slide requires a "Squash prep" method. It has to be done right because if the sample is too thick on the smear, the pathologist won't be able to see anything. Too thin, and there won't be enough sample to make a determination.

The whole thing wracked my nerves. I was just relieved that I hadn't fainted!

I returned to the lab and stained the slides then brought them to our pathologist. No bad news came out of his office later, so I must've been right. There must have been bone marrow and my slides must have been satisfactory. If not, I surely would have heard about it. Thank the Lord!

Over time, I assisted with a couple more bone marrow studies and also some spinal taps. With each one, my fascination with the procedure fortunately kept me from passing out on the floor.

***

A lab aide brought a blood sample into the lab from a pediatric outpatient for a blood cell count one morning. "Really tough draw," she said as she handed it to me. "Be extra careful with this sample. The kid wouldn't stop screaming and kicking. It took two of us to hold him while a third stuck him. Took forever to get this sample." Our aides were very skilled. If they had trouble, I was sure anybody in the world would have had a problem.

I took the precious blood and diluted it for analysis. The white cell count was high. It read 25,000. Normal is 5,000 to 10,000. The slide showed white cells all over the place. Elevated white counts can indicate an infection and have to be phoned in. I quickly called the doctor's office with the results.

A little while later in the morning, the phone rang. It was the nurse from the doctor's office. "The doctor says he doesn't believe you and wants the test to be redrawn and redone. Did you make a mistake?" Her voice sounded sarcastic. "The doctor wants you to redraw and rerun."

"Okay," I said through gritted teeth. Gee, I just loved sarcastic nurses who didn't know what they were talking about. Made my day.

How could I tell those poor lab aides that they had to draw the kicking, screaming kid again? I knew I didn't make a mistake, so it wasn't my fault, but I felt guilty. I always felt guilty. It's part of my personality.

I walked to the front of the lab where the aides congregated. I hesitated, hating to give the bad news. "Um, the doctor doesn't believe these results. He wants a new sample."

The lab aide gave me a dirty look.

Hey, I'm just the messenger.

The aide left and returned in just a few minutes. "He'd calmed down by now. We got it with no trouble," she said as she handed me the sample.

Oh, good. I didn't feel so bad then. For the aide, and for the patient.

This time, the white cell count was normal. It was obviously the Flight or Fight response system of the body activating. The body sends out lots of white cells when it thinks it's in trouble, like the little boy did when he was kicking and screaming. Then after he rested, the response returned to normal circumstances, so the body quit producing extra white cells. As a result, his count also returned to normal.

I called the doctor's office to report the findings. The nurse chuckled, "We knew a mistake had been made." She hung up before I could explain.

We didn't make a mistake. But the doctor and nurse seemed happy in thinking that "the lab made a mistake."

A common theme in medical movies is the plot point, "The lab made a mistake." Then, the fictitious patient of course is misdiagnosed and mistreated, or the wrong patient gets the medicine, causing severe illness. A smart doctor has to come along and solve the mystery. Or a compassionate nurse revives the patient back to health. I think too many people watch these movies and believe them. As a professional lab tech, this was one of my pet peeves.

If that wasn't enough, ghosts create problems in the lab for us. Well, ghost cells anyway. While doing urinalyses one morning, I looked into the microscope. The dipstick on this particular sample indicated a lot of hemoglobin present in the urine sample, the substance found inside red cells, but I didn't see any red cells under the microscope. Hmmm, must be an old sample. I turned in my report.

A nurse from the doctor's office called, saying, "The doctor says it can't be possible to have hemoglobin in the sample without you seeing any red blood cells. He wants you to repeat it."

Ah, so once again a doctor thought the lab made a mistake.

I patiently explained, "It must have been an old sample. After a few hours, the red blood cells lyse (break), releasing their hemoglobin, but because they're all lysed, we can't see them." Lab techs refer to this as 'ghost cells.' I couldn't help adding, "The doctor should have known that."

Okay, it was a little smug of me to say that, but I did get tired of some doctors being so condescending to the lab.

I could sense the nurse was taken aback. She stammered, "Oh, okay." I felt sorry for her because now she was going to have to go tell her boss that he was the one who was in the wrong. Glad I wasn't her.

Another day when I worked in the hematology department of the lab, the supervisor Ron told me, "I have to go to a management meeting," leaving me alone in the department.

Later, when I was sitting at one of our three microscopes, one of our pathologists—the lab doctor—came in, looking for a slide. Evidently, someone had requested pathologist review on a particular patient's slide. I found the one he needed and handed it to him with a smile.

Not only was it nice to have company, but I had tremendous admiration for this pathologist. Besides being a highly intelligent doctor, he was a kind man and routinely showed compassion. I respected him as a doctor and as a person.

He sat down at a microscope next to mine. After a couple minutes, his head nodded slightly and his eyes narrowed in thought. I've always envied highly intelligent people and wondered what it would be like to be that smart. Well, I'd make a lot more money, for one thing.

"What's the current diagnosis on this patient?" he asked me.

"Umm, I don't know."

"Could you call the floor and find out for me, please?" He was always polite and sweet.

Pleased to be of assistance, I dialed the floor and asked to speak to the nurse in charge of this patient. I explained who I was and what our pathologist needed.

"That's none of lab's business," the nurse said.

Excuse me? I couldn't believe my ears. *None of the lab's business?* Did I hear this ignorant person correctly? Perhaps she hadn't understood me. I explained again. "The doctor is sitting next to me and needs to know what the current diagnosis is. He's examining her slide and this information will help him evaluate what's going on with her now."

"I said, that's none of lab's business." She hung up.

I sat there stunned. Did that nurse have any idea what the role of the lab is? Did she not realize the lab is part of the team that takes care of the patient? Like the radiologist in the X-ray department, the pathologist in the lab is just one of various doctors who work together to help our patients.

Today, the Federal Government protects personal health information with HIPAA (Health Information Portability and Accountability Act of 1996). In the 1970s, patients didn't have that protection of privacy. And even today with HIPAA privacy rules, the patient's right to privacy is balanced to permit the disclosure of health information to doctors as needed for patient care.

I turned to our pathologist, the doctor for whom I had tremendous respect, and said, "The nurse says it's none of lab's business."

I expected him to be furious at the ignorant audacity of this nurse, but instead he just laughed. The ridiculousness of her comment was laughable, I guess. I suppose when you have as much self-confidence as he did, you can laugh at this type of situation. Me, I get irritated. Over the years working in the medical field, I have observed that the doctors whom I consider the best tend to have mellow personalities. Lesser doctors, especially the cocky ones, frequently have bad tempers. Lack of self-confidence, way deep-down, perhaps?

"That's okay. I have what I need to make my report." He got up and left.

I wanted to talk to that nurse's supervisor and ask her to explain to her nurse what the pathologist's role is in taking care of the patients. But I didn't. I was so busy with work that I didn't have the energy or the time. I had gotten used to the lab working together as one big team, to help patients, and many nurses worked well with the lab. I took pride in being part of the overall medical team—doctors, nurses, lab, respiratory, x-ray, etc. It surprised me when I came across a medical professional who didn't know that the lab was part of the medical team helping care for patients.

Maybe that nurse will read this book and figure it out.

***

Financially, things were much better for me on my salary as a lab tech versus when I was a student. No more rice/one apple/one vegetable for dinner. I could actually afford nice meals. I moved into a larger place in the Punchbowl area of Honolulu—the downstairs of a house. Amy and I now had separate bedrooms. A banana tree grew just outside my front door, surrounded by thick foliage. I loved living in my funky little place.

On nice days I liked to walk around the area, admiring its beauty while getting some exercise. On one of my excursions, I discovered a cute little Mom and Pop store. The first time I entered the store, the quaintness immediately struck me. One small room, candy and cookies in big glass jars on the counter, various foodstuffs on shelves, fresh fruit and vegetables in bins taking up most of the floor space. It reminded me of a little store in my small Midwestern hometown back in the Fifties.

I bought a large almond cookie. The elderly Asian proprietor reached into the glass jar with a friendly grin and took out a cookie. I also purchased some milk, bread and eggs. To my delight, he pulled out an abacus and slid the beads back and forth with practiced speed, arriving at the total.

I loved that quaint, friendly place. It immediately became my go-to store for needed items between large grocery shopping. Or when I had a yen for a soft almond cookie to melt like butter on my taste buds.

**

Jack and I continued to see each other. He remained healthy, strong, and in remission. He didn't care for going to nightclubs, but one night I talked him into it. We were lucky to get a table close to the dance floor so we could see the band. Then a waiter came over to us. "Excuse me. I was wondering if you would mind giving up your table. Tony Orlando and Dawn are here and are friends of the band and they wanted me to ask you if you would be willing to move. He'll pay for a round of drinks for you. We have a nice table further back, if that's all right with you."

We looked behind us and sure enough, Tony Orlando and Dawn stood by the door. Tony waved.

Jack and I looked at each other and nodded. We felt benevolent. "Sure. We don't care." I figured it would be a story to tell my grandchildren one day, not realizing that my future grandchildren would not know who Tony Orlando and Dawn were. Oh, well.

Jack's and my favorite entertainment involved quieter evenings. We enjoyed going to the Waikiki Shell for outdoor jazz concerts, bringing a blanket, a bottle of wine and a picnic dinner. We stretched out under the stars while allowing the music to soak into our spirits. Nights like that were truly paradise for me—a man I loved and who returned that love sitting next to me, romantic music filling my soul, looking up and gazing into the universe. It brought peace and serenity to my life. We talked about marriage. Sometimes we brought Amy with us to one of these concerts and it was like we were a family. I was content with my present and what my future would bring.

Or sometimes Jack and I walked along Waikiki Beach in the evening, holding hands, stopping to listen to a luau show behind one of the hotels. We could see and hear everything and didn't have to pay for it!

One night we drove into the country and heard the famous slack-key guitarist and singer, Gabby Pahinui, perform in a small lounge out in the country. That was a special evening, full of palpable love from the audience for his great talent. I loved small lounge shows when Hawaiian singers performed, especially at the end of the night when the audience stood in a circle holding hands listening to the final song. The Aloha Spirit filled the atmosphere.

Hawaii has no shortage of fun things to do. The state provides many lush places for hiking. Occasionally we went on nature walks, deep into the isolated semi-tropical paradise. On one excursion, after hiking quite a ways in, Jack, Amy and I realized we hadn't seen one other person all afternoon. Thick with foliage and colorful flowers, the area was like our own personal Garden of Eden. The temperature, a constant eighty degrees in Hawaii, felt warm and humid on our skin as we walked while the sun's rays succeeded in filtering through the tree branches.

We found some smooth stones to rest upon and had a drink of our water. The only sounds to break the stillness surrounding us were rustling noises as lizards scurried under nearby leaves and birds chirped as they flew from one tree to another.

We continued on our way and rounded a bend in the trail. To our delight, we discovered a small pool in front of us. Clear water from a nearby stream tumbled down a mini-waterfall, continually replenishing the nature-made pool with fresh water. The three of us stood there for a moment, taking in the almost other-worldly sight. I didn't realize God had hidden away such pockets of beauty.

We kicked off our shoes and waded in. Cool and refreshing. The water was so clear, we could see the stone-covered floor beneath.

Jack and I looked at each other, the same question in both our minds. Should we? We looked around. Not a soul in sight. We nodded.

Hawaii had a healthy attitude toward nudity and partial nudity. Unclothed toddlers frequently roamed Waikiki Beach. Maybe it was because of the many Asians living there and their history of Japanese baths where whole families bathed together. We thought nothing of saying, "Come on, Amy, let's go swimming!"

The three of us stripped down to our underpants, threw our clothes over some nearby rocks and slipped in. The water was over Amy's head in the middle but even as a young child, she was a strong swimmer.

What a great afternoon. We swam around, allowing the water to cool our skin from the heat our hiking had generated. Just the three of us in our personal paradise. The water was so pure, we could see the bottom of the pool.

And then footsteps sounded behind us. In a panic, Amy and I swam to Jack. He put his arms around both of us and we huddled together in the see-through water. That must have been how Adam and Eve felt when God found them eating the forbidden apple. Of the three of us, I was really the only one who needed to hide my body.

A couple probably in their thirties came out of the dense foliage, following the path past our pool. It was obvious the three of us only had on our underwear. The couple appeared as embarrassed as we felt. They looked away, said "Hello," grinned, and hurried past us.

That didn't stop us from enjoying our swim. They were the only people we saw all day. We hiked back to the car later, tired and happy.

Romance and platonic love are everywhere in Hawaii. You can't escape it. It's in the air all around you. You can be with a sibling, a friend, a buddy—anyone and feel the Aloha Spirit spreading its love to everybody.

Our chief tech passed around some papers at one of our monthly meetings. "Here's a list of continuing education lectures you can choose from," she said. The hospital required employees to take continuing education hours throughout the year and periodically offered lectures for us to attend if we wished.

I perused the list. There were many medical topics. The latest updates on leukemias, abnormal cell morphologies, viruses, DNA, various diseases, safety, coagulation, handling patients during a fire, etc. All subjects I had studied throughout my career ad nauseum.

My attention caught something different. Sex change operations. *Hmmmm, that might be interesting.* I signed up for that one.

On the appointed day, I walked out of the lab doors leaving work behind me one hour early at 1:30 p.m. I strolled down the hospital's auditorium for the in-service. My workday was done. All I had to do was sit back and listen, while getting paid. I loved it.

Hospital employees, mostly nurses and residents, packed the small auditorium. I found an empty seat in the middle of the tiered rows and eased into it.

The speaker was a surgeon who had performed many sex change operations. He proceeded to explain the emotional turmoil of the patients who came to him, and then the fascinating basics of the actual procedure itself, complete with slides.

He held everyone's focus and I sat riveted, listening to him. He first described how the females received functional male genitals. Then he went on to discuss the males who became women and the female parts he constructed for those patients.

When he concluded he said, "Are there any questions?"

A nurse raised her hand. "But what about the clitoris. Don't these new females get a clitoris?"

Even from a distance, I could see the surprised look spreading across the surgeon's face. Then a look of irritation replaced the surprise. He looked at the nurse for a moment and finally spoke. "What do they need a clitoris for?"

Chuckles rippled throughout the room, along with my own snicker of incredulity.

Years later, I thought of this again as I watched a Seinfeld episode, where Jerry couldn't remember a girl's name. She told him, "It rhymes with a part of the female anatomy." He finally figured out her name was Delores.

Our ongoing continuing education included our annual Medical Technology convention. The first professional medical convention I attended was held at a nice hotel in Honolulu and lasted for three days. The lab paid for our registration and also paid us a day's wages to attend. We took turns attending. The in-services were all specifically medical laboratory related and I looked forward to going.

The convention provided buffets of muffins, fruit and coffee in the mornings and a lovely luncheon at noon. I ate with some friends from KCMC lab and with some new acquaintances I had met that morning.

Another tech I worked with signed up for the same afternoon class as I had. She was Asian, married, a young mother and very quiet. Hardly ever talked. We sat waiting in the room for the instructor when a lady walked in. "May I have your attention? I'm sorry, but the instructor is sick. We will have to cancel this class. Feel free to join any other in-service today."

Shoot. We all filed out. My co-worker and I studied the brochure but didn't see any other classes that interested us. I knew my fellow lab techs were short staffed back at the hospital. I pictured them going crazy, running around trying to get through the piles of work. Disappointed, I turned to my lab friend and said, "Maybe we should go back to the lab to work for the rest of the day." I felt guilty since we were getting paid.

She looked at me as if insanity ran in my family. "Are you serious? Are you nuts? This is our day that the hospital gave us! One day a year!" The usually quiet girl had no problem in expressing her opinion. She punctuated each word and shook the brochure in my face. "We're staying! We'll find something to do."

Her adamant stance took me by surprise. Boy, for being so quiet she certainly could stand up for herself. I needed to take lessons on that. I agreed to stay.

We visited sales rep's tables, looked around, learned about new machines they were selling, and gathered free samples and goodies. After a while, we slipped away and enjoyed a glass of wine in the hotel bar.

I loved being a professional. My friend was right. We deserved this. A fine day indeed.

***

I answered my ringing phone. It was Jack.

"Will you meet me at Ala Moana Beach at 1:00? I need to talk to you," he said.

"Sure. But that doesn't give us much time for swimming. I have to pick Amy up at 3:00 from school."

"That's okay. It won't be a problem."

Happy for the surprise to unexpectedly see him that day, I changed clothes, grabbed a towel and sunscreen, and drove to Ala Moana Beach. I drove around the parking lot for fifteen minutes looking for a parking spot and ended up arriving late.

He sat on a towel at our usual place.

"Hi." I couldn't help grinning when I saw him. I spread my towel next to his and plopped down on the sandy beach.

He didn't have the usual happy expression on his face.

Worried, I asked, "Did you want to talk about something?"

His eyes held a distant look. "I'm moving to California."

Just like that.

I waited to see if he was going to ask me to move with him. Of course I would have gone. But the invitation didn't come.

Something started squeezing my heart. My stomach felt tight. I had to force myself to slow my breathing. Glad I was sitting down, I noticed things swirling around me, making me dizzy. Stunned, I finally managed to say, "When?"

"Soon."

"Why?"

"I'm moving in with my brother. I want to start a new life. I just need a change, that's all."

My whole life seemed to crash down around me. I felt like I was floundering, trying to stay above water when a current pulled at me, forcing me down. We had been together for years. Numb from the news, I asked, "Kind of sudden, isn't it?"

He shook his head. "Not really. I've been thinking about it for a while now."

"What about us?" I barely dared to ask that question, afraid of

73

the answer.

He gazed out over the ocean. "It's over. I have to move on. I just thought I should let you know."

I should think so, after four years of being nearly inseparable.

He rose, picked up his towel and turned to leave. "Good luck to you and Amy." Then he walked away.

That was the last I ever saw him.

I sat for a while staring out at the ocean. Waves broke softly against the shore. My hair fluttered in the gentle breeze that whispered past my ears. The sun's rays glittered on the water like sparkling gems. The serene and peaceful atmosphere was so at odds with my life. Didn't it know what just happened to me? How could the world ignore my turmoil? I could have sat there all day, avoiding the churning inside my soul.

But the world continued on its usual path. I lay down on my towel and soaked in the warmth of the afternoon. Laughing children ran past me. The ocean's saltwater scent mixed with the smell of Coppertone, a smell I loved. I tried to feel some happiness.

My mind had a difficult time accepting what just happened. I sighed and rose, having to go pick up Amy. As time went by, the reality sunk in. I didn't feel angry—just depressed. I moped around and didn't eat very much. My stomach couldn't handle food. All I wanted to do was sleep but I had to move on. Go to work. Pay the bills. Pick up Amy from school. At least I had her. I don't know what I would have done if I hadn't had Amy to cheer me up. Her delightful fun personality injected joy into my days.

My life flipped upside down. When I went to a cute, funny romantic comedy with Amy where the entire audience laughed, I looked around the theater and saw couples holding hands, enjoying the humorous movie. But it depressed me. It only served as a reminder that the whole world had a romantic relationship except me. Or it seemed like that anyway. Liz had a boyfriend. Linda was a mother and married to a lawyer.

And then I went to work where sick, dying children surrounded me and I felt happy because my child was healthy. Depressed at a romantic comedy movie, happy that someone else's child instead of mine was dying? I was sick in the head. I disgusted myself.

I was having landlord problems at the time and I wanted to

move to a nicer neighborhood. Grabbing a pen and paper, I sat down and wrote out a budget to calculate how much rent I could afford. Apartments were extremely expensive in Honolulu. I got a Sunday paper and searched through the rental ads in my spending range.

"No children allowed." "No children or pets allowed." "No pets, no children allowed." That's all I saw. My salary wasn't high enough to purchase a home by myself in Hawaii. Rents continually climbed and my paycheck couldn't keep up. I didn't think I could afford to stay there any longer. Also, I came from a big family and my by now ten-year-old daughter was growing up without seeing much of her cousins or grandparents. It was summer of 1980. After almost eight years on the beautiful islands, loved them as I did, I felt the time had come to finally return to the mainland.

I went to the beach alone to do some thinking. When I first arrived in Honolulu in January, 1973, I could see the mountains on the other side of Waikiki Beach when my back was to the ocean.

Things had changed over the years and real estate in Honolulu was prime. Now, buildings worked their way up the sides of the mountains. Tall complexes rose along Kalakaua Boulevard, blocking any view of the mountains from the beach. The view now consisted only of the clouds and mist hovering around the mountain peaks. Over the years I heard various people complain of "Island Fever" but it never attacked me. I didn't mind living on a small island, always keeping busy and having fun. That wasn't my reason for deciding to leave.

Where did I want to move? I prayed for guidance. Although I had been raised in Minnesota, Hawaii's year-round sunshine and clear skies had spoiled me. I didn't relish returning to the blustery winters of the Midwest. The weather in sunny Arizona, where one of my sisters had settled and where my parents spent the winters now, attracted me.

I sold my old VW for the same price I had paid for it five years prior, packed up my things, bought plane tickets to Phoenix, sent Amy on ahead of me to my sister's and said my tearful good-byes to friends.

I cried as the plane crossed the Pacific, knowing I would always miss Hawaii, its beauty and its friendly people. Leaving my dear friends after all those years hit me hard. Would my heart heal from losing Jack? Would I ever see my girlfriends again?

Even though I knew the cost of living in Arizona was much lower than in Hawaii, I still wondered: Would I be able to make enough money to provide a good life for the two of us? Would I get a job I liked? Would Amy adjust to a new school and make new friends all right? Would we be happy? These questions weighed heavily on my heart as a new phase in our lives began.

I would miss Jack. I would miss my friends. I would miss the beauty and Aloha spirit pervading the islands which had become home to me. Tears rolled down my face.

A woman across the aisle in the plane leaned over with a worried look on her face and asked, "Are you all right? Is there anything I can do?"

I didn't realize I'd been crying that loudly.

With my heart crushed, I gazed out the plane's window, remembering how Amy had thought the kwowds (clouds) had fallen down on our way over, seven-and-a-half years earlier. This time, I didn't feel above the clouds. In spite of being in a plane, I felt like I had been dragged way below any cloud. Jack, Amy and I had become family over the years. I couldn't figure out what had happened.

It wasn't until after I settled in Arizona that I discovered the reason for his actions.

Clint Eastwood and me

Queen Kapiolani

Amy, me, and Dad at Pearl Harbor

Amy at Waikiki Beach

Amy and me in our Honolulu apartment

Me with Liz at Ala Moana Beach

A friend, Linda, and me holding Amy

Me with my parents and Amy on the Big Island wearing
tourist hats. 1974

My parents with Amy on Diamond Head Road. 1974

Me enjoying a day at Waikiki Beach

PART THREE
ARIZONA AND EMERGENCY CENTERS

When Amy and I first arrived in Arizona, we stayed with one of my sisters, Kathie, her husband and their two daughters—two of Amy's many cousins. Moving and facing all the changes that accompany moving, made me anxious. Almost eight years before, when we moved to Hawaii, I wasn't nervous at all. It had been a fun adventure. I was young then and adventurous. This time proved different, however.

My face broke out from the stress. I didn't know if I could handle all the changes in our lives. I was losing my nerve. Thirty one-years-old now, I found it difficult to re-capture the free-spirit of my youth that had surged through me so easily when I was twenty-three. All I could do was put one foot in front of the other and get things done, leaning on God to help us.

The intensity of Phoenix's daytime heat shocked me. I had visited Phoenix before but in the wintertime. I was unprepared for how hot the summer temperatures were.

My savings account contained a little bit of money so my first project involved finding an apartment. Raised in a small town in Minnesota, then living on an island with limited space, the vastness of Phoenix and the valley surrounding it took some getting used to. Kathie had a blue Pinto station wagon. She drove the kids and me around looking at apartments. I sat up front with Kathie. Amy and her two cousins, ages eight and six, put the back seat down so they could spread out.

The Pinto had an air conditioner, but the one-hundred-and-fifteen degree temperature outside bore down on her car like a fire. I tried to direct the thin stream of coolish air toward the back for the kids. Trickles of sweat dripped down the sides of their beet-red faces. They fanned themselves with folded pieces of paper. They looked miserable but not one word of complaint left their lips. Despite their pitiful looks of discomfort, my nieces' eyes carried determination to help their Auntie and cousin find a home. So sweet! My supportive family helped calm my nerves.

I bought an old car and applied for jobs. While waiting for a phone call and interview, I spent a lot of time at my sister's. Jumping into their pool helped Amy and me deal with the heat. Pool parties, barbecues, croquet in the evenings at their house, made the transition easier for Amy and me.

Amy was happy to be near her family. I was glad my daughter was getting to know her cousins. She had spent too many years miles away from family. I finally relaxed, realizing I had made the right decision to move to Arizona.

After a few days, we found an apartment I could afford in Phoenix. I once again met other single mothers in my apartment building to exchange babysitting duties. Amy made new friends easily.

Through phone calls from friends and his brother in Denver, I soon learned what happened to Jack. His cancer, Hodgkin's Disease, had returned. After all those years of being in remission, it had finally come back and beaten him. He'd passed away.

Liz, my friend in Hawaii, said to me, "He must not have wanted to put you through that. He probably knew it was best for you and Amy to get on with your lives as soon as possible."

She was right, of course, but it still made me horribly sad. And angry that I couldn't be there for him. Hurt that I found out from someone else other than him. And devastated because I missed him terribly.

I kept myself busy so I didn't think of him every waking moment. When I told Amy the bad news, she was upset also. Fortunately, children are resilient. All we could do was look to our future we had already begun. Jack was right. It had been better for us to get on with our lives right away without him. It made the news easier to bear. He was one smart guy. But I still thought about him and missed him.

It took a while for me to adjust to not only the heat, but also the culture in Phoenix. It was different than what I was used to. In Hawaii, people were fascinated by the different ethnic traits. One of the first questions people asked in Hawaii was, "What ethnic group do you belong to?" Japanese, Chinese, Filipino, Polynesian, Okinawan—everyone got along together. They were proud of their heritage and enjoyed discussing it.

In Arizona, I quickly learned it was considered impolite to discuss or ask about one's ethnic background, something I found very strange. Shouldn't everybody own pride in their heritage?

In September, Amy attended public school two blocks from our apartment building. A man walked into her room. The teacher was at the front of the room at the blackboard, her back to the room. She heard nervous laughter and looked around. There stood a man at the door, exposing himself. Amy was in the back of the room and couldn't see much, fortunately.

The man ran out. The teacher went outside and screamed. That got the attention of a male teacher next door who took off running after the guy. He didn't catch him. The guy was never found.

The school sent a notice to all the parents about the incident. It shocked me. In all the years Amy had attended school in Hawaii, nothing like that had ever happened.

I also discovered an unnerving statistic: the crime rate in Phoenix was much higher than in Hawaii. Since I had worked in the Rape Center in Honolulu, it seemed like there was a lot of rape there, but the numbers proved differently. It was worse in Arizona.

This made me nervous, especially as a single mother. I felt vulnerable. I missed the Aloha Spirit so prevalent in Hawaii. But having family a few miles away helped ease my fear.

***

I found a job not too far from my apartment building. It was in what the owner, a hospital across town called Phoenix Desert Hospital, referred to as a "free-standing emergency center." Other than one doctor and one receptionist, the emergency center staffed one nurse, one x-ray tech, and one lab tech per shift—a skeleton crew. Since the center's staff consisted of only five people at a time, the hospital cross-trained the lab and x-ray techs to help the center's nurse. The hospital owned three free-standing emergency centers and I rotated between all three of them at one time or another.

I learned how to assist doctors as they sutured, take vital signs, mini-catheterize for urine samples, do EKG's, give tetanus shots, set up and administer medicinal breathing treatments, tend to paronychias, apply plaster splints and other duties. Cool! I loved the opportunity to expand my knowledge and enjoyed learning First-Aid. I still performed lab tests but also interacted with patients in ways I never had before. However, I missed the camaraderie of other lab techs around me to "talk lab" with. My job now required a balance of lab and helping the nurse, providing a different challenge. I was totally up for it.

When I first walked into the Emergency Center, resentment from the staff was thick in the air, palpable on my skin. They evidently didn't like new people. The staff had worked together as a team for a long time and didn't care for change. I knew I would have to prove myself to them.

The training period at Deer Valley Emergency Center was an odd experience. One week, the nurse on that shift totally ignored me. Instead of training me to assist the nurses, she turned her back on me and alphabetized the filing system—something she probably had never done in all the years she had worked there.

The next week, the nurse from the other shift was quite cold and distant, with a definite anger emanating from her. I later learned she had recently experienced every Emergency Room employee's nightmare. The door had burst open one night and some people carried in a full-code. No heartbeat. It turned out to be her husband.

My source told me she totally freaked and threw herself around his feet while he was carried to a bed. She evidently became hysterical, screaming. Since she was the only nurse there, the doctor handled the code by himself with help from the x-ray tech and lab tech. The man didn't make it. So I forgave her for not being friendly. She had a lot to deal with emotionally.

The other employees were territorial of their space and didn't want new people invading their private world. It was as if they were sending me a silent message—'This is our place and you'd better do things our way.' I wasn't used to this attitude. Kapiolani Hospital had welcomed me right from the beginning.

What did I get myself into? But the money was good. I was already committed and I enjoyed the work itself. I needed the job and couldn't afford to quit and look for something else. Finally I finished training and then worked 8:00 to 8:00, seven days on, seven days off. I loved my schedule. It gave me lots of days off work to be at home with Amy. Plus, it gave me overtime each pay period, allowing me to earn the extra money I badly required.

On one of my first days at the emergency center, a one-year-old child came in who had a cut on his chin. "Okay, big boy, come on back," I said as his mother carried him across the linoleum floor.

Chart in hand, I led them to a vacant bed. I took the youngster's vital signs: blood pressure, temperature, pulse and respiration rate, then asked all the medical history questions.

The doctor came over and examined the boy. "His chin needs stitches. Set up a suture tray and put him in a papoose board," she said to me.

Using the sterile technique I had learned in training, I prepared a sterile suture tray at the bedside for the doctor. Then I grabbed a papoose board and placed it on the bed.

Hmm. How do I use this thing? We hadn't covered this in my training. I examined the contraption. Four flaps of blue material with Velcro® on them. The two upper flaps each had a hole. I stood there holding the flaps, staring at the holes. Various scenarios ran through my head. Other patients kept the other employees occupied so I couldn't ask them.

The holes must be for the arms, I decided. Duh. Obvious.

The mother held her son in her arms, patiently waiting. Embarrassed I didn't know what to do, I decided to plunge ahead. The doctor sat in the nurse's station waiting.

I placed the baby on his back on the board and wrapped the two lower flaps around his legs and velcroed them tightly into place. So far, so good. I eased each of his arms through the holes in the two upper flaps, then velcroed those flaps together around his torso, under his arms. I stood back and proudly surveyed my handiwork, smiling broadly.

The doctor moved with small, quick strides over to the bedside, ready to suture. Energy radiated from her short stature. In the little time since I had met her, I could tell she liked things to progress quickly.

She stopped and stared. The child's arms flailed wildly in the air. The doctor glared at me like she couldn't believe me. She rolled her eyes and shook her head.

Why is she looking at me like that, I wondered.

Then in a flash, it came to me. Oops. The arms should be strapped underneath the material! Feeling stupid, I said, "Um, I'll fix it."

The doctor stomped off in a huff.

Stupid, stupid, stupid. Positive that my face burned red from embarrassment, I unfastened the two upper flaps, gently pulled the boy's arms out of the holes, then wrapped the material around him and velcroed them back into place. The child couldn't move from his neck down to his ankles. He screamed in protest.

I held the boy's head still while the doctor stitched his chin. She didn't say one word to me. After that, she refused to work at any of Phoenix Desert Hospital's three emergency centers ever again, only accepting shifts at the hospital's emergency room across town. She wasn't well liked, so our little staff should actually have thanked me for my ignorance of papoose boards!

***

My parents drove down to live in Phoenix during the cold Minnesota winter months—snowbirds. They helped me, often watching Amy on the weekends I worked. I took a second job on my days off for a while, also, working in a doctor's office, performing lab tests, mostly gram stains. I saved the extra money to plunk down a down-payment on a townhouse for Amy and me. I felt guilty leaving her for that length of time, but it had to be done. We needed more than just my one salary. It seemed like I was always tired. I had two choices: either get welfare help and have more time to be a mother, or, work my butt off, work a second job, and support us with no assistance but be gone from home a lot. It was a difficult decision but I felt I had to choose the latter.

I eventually found a little townhouse to purchase, down the street from where my parents stayed in the winters. One evening I curled up into a comfortable chair upstairs and read. Amy was staying overnight at my parents' place to visit. A loud crash downstairs startled me. I looked at the clock. It was ten p.m. Kind of frightened, I inched my way down the stairs and looked around the first floor. I didn't see anybody.

Then I noticed a picture of my daughter and me, taken in Hawaii, had fallen off the wall onto the floor. The nail was still on the wall. The flap on the back of the picture frame was still attached. There was no reason for that picture to fall. I stood alone in the dark quiet room, waiting. For a flash of a second, I sensed someone there. Then the feeling vanished.

The next day, I asked Amy, "Just wondering if anything weird happened to you last night at Grandpa's?" I didn't mention yet what had happened to me.

She told me she had been trying to find something in a closet and couldn't find it.. Explaining what happened, she said, "I said out loud, 'Oh, I wish someone would help me find this!' Just then, it fell off the top shelf and landed right in front of me!"

Hmmm. Strange. "Do you remember what time that was?"

"Yeah, right after ten o'clock because I had just finished watching T.V."

Two strange things happening to Amy and me simultaneously, involving a picture of us taken in Hawaii, and Amy receiving assistance when she needed it. Could it have been Jack, reaching across from another world to tell us he was watching over us? I've told this to various people and nobody believes it. Not even Amy. You probably don't believe it either. But the thought comforted me.

I realized it was time to let go of Jack. He was in a better place and wanted us to move on.

***

In 1980, our blood gas machine was not a fancy self-calibrating one. Gases are volatile, so we had to calibrate the machine manually throughout the day.

When I had been in training, the center's other lab tech showed me large bottles of standards for calibrating kept in the cupboard above the machine, next to various other reagents. There were two large bottles—a high standard and a low. They were just like the ones we used in Hawaii. I squirted out a small amount of the low standard into a tiny cup and held it up to the machine to be aspirated. Then I dialed various knobs, forcing the machine to read that exact value. Then I repeated the procedure using the high standard.

I went back and forth doing this until the machine read those exact values without having to touch any dials. Then I checked its accuracy by running three levels of controls. In Hawaii, we made our own gas controls, but here we purchased them, which was nice.

After I began working on my own, I came on duty one day and the other lab tech took off quickly, eager to get home to her husband and life. We each worked twelve-hour shifts, splitting the twenty-four hours a day. Immediately afterwards, our ER doc ordered a blood gas on a patient who just came in. I zipped back to the gas machine to calibrate it. I reached up into the cupboard to get the standard bottles, but they weren't there. Other reagents for various other machines sat on the shelves but not the two large bottles of gas standards I needed right then. I saw the controls, but not the standards which were absolutely necessary.

Frantically I searched everywhere, flinging open all the cupboard doors, running from one cupboard to the next. It was a fairly large lab and had lots of cupboards. I looked behind all our machines on the countertops, yanked open drawers and rummaged through them. Nothing.

Now what should I do? I forced myself not to panic.

I had no one to call. People in the lab at Phoenix Desert Hospital had never stepped foot in our little center and wouldn't know anything about our particular lab. And I didn't have a phone number for my fellow emergency center lab tech who had just left.

I had to tell our doctor I couldn't run the test because I couldn't find the standard bottles. I felt like an idiot.

He fumed. This particular doctor walked around like he thought he was better than everyone else. He talked about opera and classic literature as if he were the only patron of the arts on earth. I love classical music also, but that didn't phase him. And to add to his charm, he reeked of B.O. I didn't want this guy on my bad side. Someone had told me he was extremely religious, so I hoped he would be forgiving and give me another chance instead of getting me into trouble with my boss at the main lab.

Fortunately, no other patient came in requiring an arterial blood gas test that day. When the other tech came back to work twelve hours later, I related the problem to her.

"Oh, we switched companies. We don't use those bottles anymore. The new standards came in last night." She walked over to a cupboard and opened the door. She showed me a small plastic box of tiny glass ampoules. "These are the new ones."

Came in yesterday?? So why didn't she bother to tell me? My teeth clenched so hard my jaw ached as my mind tried to absorb what she said.

She turned away from me and stomped around the lab. Evidently I had been dismissed. Not wishing to create any bad vibes between us, I didn't pursue the matter. She had worked for the hospital for years and I was the new one. So I simply said, "Okay," and went home.

Later, my home phone rang. The voice of the chief tech in our main lab at Phoenix Desert Hospital came across the line. "I just had a call from one of the ER doctors. He said you were unable to do a blood gas. He wants you to have more training."

Oh great. One of my first shifts on my own and there's already a complaint about me. My glance fell on my ASCP pin sitting on a table next to the phone. I swallowed hard. All that studying and experience wasn't doing me a bit of good.

"It wasn't my fault," I defended myself. "I couldn't find the standards. Evidently we switched standards the previous day and the other tech didn't tell me. I was looking for large bottles but they're tiny ampoules now. I didn't recognize them as standards."

"The responsibility to ask if something is new is incumbent upon yourself. It's not up to the other tech to tell you if something has changed," he said, irritation emanating from his voice and shooting across the phone line straight into my heart.

The responsibility...is incumbent upon yourself? *What? Is this guy for real??* I didn't know what to think of him. "You mean, I'm supposed to come in every single day and ask if anything new happened? Instead of the tech just telling me whenever there's something different?"

"Yes. That's what I mean."

Oh for Pete's sake. That was the craziest thing I had ever heard. I let out a big sigh. Nothing I could do now but kiss ass. This ass-kissing business was getting old. Kiss-ass the doctors. Kiss-ass the other lab tech. Kiss-ass the chief tech at the hospital. "Okay. I will."

Fortunately, nothing like this happened again and my boss didn't make me go through training again. Perhaps the other lab tech had stuck up for me—a definite possibility. If she did, I'm grateful.

***

At the age of thirty-one, I led a more settled life than I had in my twenties in Hawaii. Church, family, new friends, and work kept me busy. I worked my second job for a few months until I had some money saved and then quit. I was exhausted. Now, my seven days off were like a mini-vacation twice a month. Amy and I could get used to that schedule!

A female patient in her twenties came into the center and our doctor had to do a pelvic exam on her. I had not worked with this particular doctor before. Donning sterile gloves, I assisted and laid out the instruments. I stood next to the patient's bed while the doctor examined the patient. Finally, he turned to me and said, "I'll need a wet'n'dry."

A wet'n'dry? What the hell's he talking about? I had never heard of such a thing. I didn't want to appear ignorant but I had to ask because he sat there expectantly, like he wanted me to get something for him.

Finally I got the nerve to ask, "What's a 'wet'n'dry'?"

His jaw dropped and his eyes narrowed. He looked at me like he couldn't believe what he just heard. He craned his neck to look at my ID badge then said in a sarcastic voice, "You are lab, aren't you?"

My ID badge clearly stated "Lab." I held my temper and tried to sound nonplussed. "Yes, but I've never heard that term before." Perhaps it was an Arizona phrase?

His eyes rolled and he sighed. "It's a wet mount and a gram stain. You do know what those are, don't you?" he asked through gritted teeth, not bothering to hide his sarcasm.

Aha! A wet mount and a gram stain! Now he's talking my language! Why didn't he say that in the first place? Those are the professional names of the laboratory tests he wanted. I wasn't familiar with the little nicknames he had for laboratory tests.

Now it was my turn to speak through gritted teeth, indicating

91

my irritation. "Yes, of course." From a patient's standpoint, he was a good doctor and the patients received good care from him, but from my standpoint he was a jerk. Most of the other ER doctors I had briefly met up to that point seemed very nice. I just had to get used to the occasional rude one. I handed him a slide, a sterile cotton tipped swab, and a test tube containing pre-measured saline. He collected the sample and then I went into the lab, stained the slide, and examined the two specimens microscopically. I handed my report to the doctor. Nothing was ever said about the incident again.

The next few times I worked with that doctor, he was nice to me. I came to realize many medical professionals don't have patience with new people. They're perfectionists and also want everything accomplished quickly. Once the new person is acclimated and picks up speed, knowing where everything is located and used to the specific manner in which things are done there, and the nicknames various individuals used instead of professional jargon, then that new person is accepted. My co-workers eventually began to respect me professionally.

Facing challenges at work and beating them made me feel proud of myself. That feeling became addicting. Anything less than a challenge became boring. I needed that excitement and thrived on it. However, I was getting tired of constantly having to prove myself.

I'm also a perfectionist but I made sure in the future to always treat new people with kindness and patience. I vowed never to forget what it was like being new. Various new employees over the years said to me, "You're the only person here who's nice to me." I could certainly relate to that feeling.

***

All different types of patients came to the emergency center, providing lots of variety to my job. A nice-looking sixty-year-old female patient came in late one night, bleeding. She was post-menopausal. She had had intercourse and afterwards started bleeding. Her husband brought her in. Our ER doctor performed a pelvic exam on her. She was torn and hemorrhaging, which can happen to post-menopausal women due to lack of lubrication.

Besides the patient, I also felt sorry for the poor husband. Guilt covered his face even though it wasn't his fault. He paced up and down the hall, obviously very agitated. When he sat next to his wife, he touched her hand in a very gentle and loving manner. He looked like he was going to cry.

Our doctor packed her internally to contain the bleeding and called a gynecologist to arrange meeting the patient at Phoenix Desert Hospital's ER for specialized treatment to stop the bleeding.

I gave the woman written instructions which basically consisted of, "Go straight to Phoenix Desert Hospital emergency room to meet the specialist." I gave them the doctor's name. Before she left, she went into the restroom located in the hallway next to the row of beds.

Just then the front door burst open and three men rushed in, carrying an unconscious twenty- two-year-old male. He had collapsed while working a construction job. They heaved him onto an empty bed next to the restroom and we immediately got to work. The nurse started an IV. The x-ray tech attached a monitor to his chest. I connected an oxygen mask to the wall, adjusted the flow to high and situated it on his face. The doctor inserted a catheter into his chest, then handed me an unheparinized glass syringe full of arterial blood, ordering, "Blood gas!"

Heparin is necessary to keep the blood from clotting. Even a tiny clot will distort the values, not to mention clog up my machine; that is if I could even get a clotted mess out of the syringe in the first place. Oh, why hadn't that doctor let me put heparin in the syringe first?

I gripped the glass syringe and ran to the back. Every second mattered. We had been busy and I hadn't had time to calibrate my blood gas machine since the beginning of my shift three hours before. I needed to calibrate the machine manually because gases are volatile, but first I grabbed a bottle of heparin and another glass syringe to heparinize the sample the doctor gave me. Silently I cursed the doctor for handing me a sample that hadn't been heparinized but I suppose he figured he didn't have time to wait for me to heparinize a syringe. He was obviously unaware of the problem it would cause me.

Transferring the patient's blood to a heparinized syringe was not easy to do because the blood couldn't be exposed to the air for even a milli-second and the bottom of glass syringes slip out easily. Before I could accomplish this task, the x-ray tech ran into the lab in a panic. "The oxygen in the wall ran out! We have to switch oxygen tanks! I don't know how to do that! Do you?"

Uh, no, I didn't. I had only been working there a few weeks at the time. I had never switched large oxygen tanks in my life. Without oxygen, the patient could die. I looked at the blood sample which quickly needed to be heparinized so it wouldn't turn into a clotted mess. Time had already slipped by. I looked at my blood gas machine which needed to calibrate. My glance moved to the x-ray tech, back at the blood sample, over to my machine, and back to the x-ray tech.

I made my decision. "Let's go."

We ran into the storage room in the back of the center. Two huge oxygen tanks, each bigger than I was, stood against a wall. One was hooked up to tubing that came out of the wall, supplying the oxygen masks with its precious gas. Pliers hung on the other tank.

I had no idea what to do, but there was no time to think. I turned one knob, twisted another, handed the x-ray tech a gadget, pulled at something, tightened something else, and somehow, I'm not sure how, got the oxygen flowing through the wall to the patient's mask again.

Then I bolted out of the storage room back to the lab, praying the blood sample hadn't clotted. Holding my breath so my hands didn't move, I carefully and slowly transferred the patient's blood into the new glass syringe which was slippery from the heparin. Please, God, don't let it clot.

It worked. No clots!

And not one light on the blood gas machine flashed red at me when the calibration finished. Thank God! They were a steady green. This meant it had calibrated correctly and was ready to go. I opened the flap-door and slowly pushed the sample out of the slippery glass syringe until the sensor stopped it. When numbers started flashing on the screen, I filled out the requisition as fast as I could, and ran back up the hallway to hand it to the doctor.

The nurse stood on a stool doing chest compressions on the boy. The receptionist had called an ambulance to come transfer him to Phoenix Desert Hospital.

The x-ray tech assisted the doctor, handing him items he required. The nurse was getting tired. I offered to take her place compressing the boy's chest. Before I took one step, the door to the restroom opened and the hemorrhaging lady's head peeked out.

She hadn't left yet to meet the gynecologist?

"Excuse me," she politely said as she sat on the commode, "but some of my packing fell out. It's dangling down into the toilet. I don't dare get up. I'm bleeding badly." Her husband stood near the door, wringing his hands, a helpless look on his pale face.

Heaven help her! I imagined her hemorrhaging to death in our bathroom while we busied ourselves just a few feet away. I walked towards her to see what I could do, when the receptionist's voice called out, "Chest pain! Bed 2!" I turned and saw her helping an elderly man onto the bed. Sweat dripped off his forehead. A pained expression covered his face.

I looked at him, turned and surveyed the lady on the commode, then glanced back at the twenty-two-year-old patient being worked on by our one doctor, nurse and x-ray tech, then looked at the old man again. I said to the lady, "Uh, I'll be right back."

While my co-workers handled the young man who was coding, I hooked the elderly gentleman to a heart monitor, gave him some oxygen, took his vitals, got an EKG on him, and asked all the necessary questions, writing furiously. I knew I'd have a load of blood work to do on him—cardiac enzymes, Chem 7 panel, CBC, possibly even a blood gas.

I finally got a scissors to the lady in the bathroom so she could cut the packing strips that were hanging down. She finally left for the hospital accompanied by her husband.

The ambulance arrived to transfer the coding young man to Phoenix Desert Hospital. Later, the doctor called the hospital and we learned he had a congenital heart defect. He died at the hospital, a sad ending for him and his family.

The elderly gentleman's x-ray, and the multiple blood tests I had performed, all turned out to be normal. Heartburn. He went home.

We heard the woman made it just fine to Phoenix Desert Hospital to meet the specialist and was well taken care of.

After all the patients had left, we cleaned up all the messes and somehow got through the rest of our shift, exhausted and deflated from the news of the boy's death, but knowing he had received the best of care.

As I helped clean, a warm feeling came over me. Where did that come from? It was then I realized for the first time that I truly felt part of their team. A member of the emergency center. Even though we had lost a patient, we had helped others and done our best. The staff was committed to helping patients and my respect for them grew. The respect became mutual.

I loved helping patients. The rest was always in God's hands. I liked being part of that team and overcoming challenges. It was a good feeling.

***

I learned a lot about collecting specimens while working in the emergency centers. I mini-cathed females for urine samples, which was a challenge just like finding a vein. I should have catheterized male patients also but somehow I always managed to be working on a different patient when a male needed to be catheterized. *Sorry. Busy. Can't do that right now. Get the nurse.* A new respect for nurses grew inside me as I watched them perform their multiple tasks with skill and caring.

What would my fellow lab techs in laboratories across the country think? Not many of them had ever mini-cathed a patient in their lives, I was sure. Nurses performed this duty. Although many lab techs didn't like patient contact—that's why they chose to work in a lab—I liked it most of the time and found it rewarding.

I zipped around helping my co-workers and also performing my own laboratory duties.

A twenty-year-old girl came in one night complaining of pain and burning while voiding her bladder. A doctor I hadn't met before worked that shift. This doctor covered his overweight body by wearing loose, slovenly looking clothes. He also bossed everyone around. I took an immediate dislike to him. "I need to do a pelvic exam on the patient," he said.

Everyone else looked busy so I assisted. I got everything ready and stood by the bedside. The doctor came into the tiny room, closed the door, donned some gloves and sat down on a stool at the foot of the bed. He took one look at the patient and backed away, pushing his stool against the wall with his feet. He made a distasteful face and said, "Yuck! You've got herpes!" He stood up, snapped off his gloves, tossed them into the waste can, turned to me and said, "Get a culture," then walked out the door.

Collecting a genital culture sample was his job! I didn't appreciate him shoving his responsibility onto me. But I had no choice. The patient lay there, needing help.

The girl started to cry softly. "My fiancé must be running around on me. I wondered why I felt this burning." She buried her face in her hands as she lay on the table. I felt sorry for her. The doctor had no decent bedside manner. What a way to find out you have herpes!

I sighed, put on some gloves, grabbed a culturette, and tried to find a good spot on her to culture. Afterwards, the patient used the restroom. As soon as she exited the restroom, another lady slipped in. I wanted to shout to the second lady, "Be sure to line the toilet seat!" but the door closed quickly and I was on the other end of the room at the time so I couldn't.

I tried to imagine what my friends working in the lab in Hawaii would think about collecting this herpes sample. I remembered hearing the following story. A mother brought her baby into the outpatient lab for a stool culture. The baby had diarrhea in its diaper. The aides didn't want to collect the sample and none of the techs did either. All they had to do was take a culturette and stick it in the diaper to get some of the stool sample. Big deal. Finally, a microbiology lab tech said, "Oh, I'll do it."

Since I was collecting all types of cultures now and performing all types of procedures, I knew I'd certainly come a long ways!

***

Seven days off every other week. What a glorious work schedule I had! At Christmastime, another of my three sisters who lived in Minnesota flew down to Arizona to visit us with her two children. My parents took all of us to Disneyland—their five grandchildren, my two sisters, me and themselves. We had a blast. I'd never been there before. My parents were like that—always

97

generous with their time and money to help any of their six kids, even though they were not wealthy people in the least.

Amy got into AGS, Arizona Girls Softball—an organization her two younger cousins played in. I had played slow-pitch softball when I was young in Minnesota and had a lot of fun. AGS was fast-pitch. A couple of those girls were clocked pitching at seventy miles per hour. Tall and strong for her age, Amy displayed a natural talent for batting. On my days off work, I watched her practices and exciting games. She played second base and sometimes outfield. I brought a folding chair, a cooler of beverages, and enjoyed Arizona's warm spring days while cheering for her team. Eventually I became team mother and scorekeeper.

It was hard not to get caught up in the fast-paced games. The opposing team's catcher threw a ball to third base as our runner neared the plate. The other team's third baseman was a full foot off the base and never tagged our runner. The umpire called our runner out. My chair was situated by third base and I witnessed the entire bad call. I jumped out of my chair and yelled, "Are you blind? She was a foot away from that base! The runner's safe!" A metal fence surrounding the field kept me from getting too close to that stupid umpire who refused to change the call. We got gypped.

At another game with a different umpire, Amy hit a homerun and rounded the bases. The umpire said, "She didn't touch second base."

"Tag her! Tag her!" The opponents screamed to their catcher who complied.

Amy later told me she knew she touched second because she pushed off it with her foot as she ran. Jerk umpire.

In the middle of one of her annual seasons, Amy slid into second and hurt her ankle. She hopped off the field and I took her to the ER where they diagnosed a break and treated it with a splint until the swelling went down. Out for the rest of the season. Bummer. Another girl that night also slid into second and also broke her ankle. The umpire found a small mound of dirt by the plate the girls were sliding into that twisted their feet back. He leveled the ground and no one else got hurt.

Southern Minnesota where I grew up had its own beauty— the lakes, green rolling hills, precisely laid-out farmland. Hawaii of course was gorgeous with its beaches, ocean, red dirt and mountains lush with green vegetation. But the desert's mild winters and beautiful scenery grew on me. I loved being outdoors in Phoenix.

My widowed aunt came to Arizona to visit. My whole family drove up to Sedona with her on a day trip. Sedona's beauty, with its red rock, bright blue skies and gorgeous mountains, rivaled Hawaii's beauty.

We also traveled to Prescott with a visiting sister from Minnesota. Prescott reminded me of small towns in Minnesota, with its pine trees and Midwestern-looking houses as opposed to Phoenix's cacti and Southwestern style homes with red tile roofs. In Prescott, we visited museums of the former capital's memorabilia and walked up and down Whiskey Row window shopping.

I was beginning to find Arizona a beautiful state also, with many fun places to go and things to do for Amy and me, including seeing the awesome and breathtaking grandeur of the Grand Canyon.

One spring day, my sister Kathie drove her two daughters, Amy and me down through the Tucson desert to Old Tucson where many movies have been filmed. Re-enacted gun shootouts entertained us. We walked around under the blazing sun, occasionally catching a glimpse of a lizard quickly scurrying away from us. The scent of blooming spring desert wildflowers wafted through the air. I bought some prickly pear jelly made from the prickly pear cactus. We also went to Tucson's Desert Museum.

On our way back, Kathie's blue Pinto station wagon wove through the Sonoran Desert on a gravel path through the rocky dry ground in wide-open spaces as we enjoyed the splendor of the desert and its endless saguaro cacti. The Sonoran Desert is the only place in the world where the Saguaro cactus grows in the wild. It was a long drive and we were all hot and tired. After a while, each desert scene looked just like the last desert scene and we became anxious to get home.

We passed two old men camping in the desert, sitting in chairs drinking beer. They waved to us. We waved back.

For the next hour, we continued to drive through the desert, passing one saguaro cactus after another, talking about the day, sipping our water bottles. We drove and drove through the desert, both Kathie and me navigating to get to the I-10 to return to

Phoenix. Teamwork.

Tired, I looked out the window and saw two old men camping in the desert, sitting in chairs drinking beer. They waved.

What? "Um, Kathie, look! It's those same old two men we saw an hour ago! I think we've been going in a circle," I said.

We waved back.

This time around, we paid more attention to our turns as we wound our way through the desert and finally reached the I-10.

***

A monitor screen in the employee lounge at the emergency center displayed people entering and exiting our front doors. On one quiet afternoon, the door beeped and our heads turned to the monitor. A young man walked in. This one was my turn, so I walked up front to wait for the receptionist to finish the chart.

By the time I got to the front, the man was already on his way out the door. Why was he leaving? Curious, I rounded the corner and walked toward him.

He looked to be in his early twenties, tall, thin, blond, a good -looking guy in blue jeans and white t-shirt.

"Can I help you?" I asked.

He turned toward me and I was startled to see one of his eyes looked horribly infected. I'm not an expert on this matter but it was so bad, even an inexperienced person like myself could tell he needed medical attention. And fast.

"There's something wrong with my eye."

"Why don't you go back and get checked in and then we'll take care of it for you."

He shifted his weight from one leg to the other and looked at the floor. "I can't. I'm homeless. I live in the field in the back. The lady said she couldn't check me in if I didn't have an address."

I glanced at our receptionist. She sat filing her nails, not paying any more attention to him. I wasn't going to argue with her. This boy needed attention. There was no way I would allow him to walk out the door.

"Follow me." I led him back to the eye exam room. I took his vital signs—blood pressure, temperature, respiratory rate—then asked him all the necessary medical questions. Was he allergic to

100

any medications? Was he on any meds? How much did he weigh? Any medical history? He was quiet, polite and cooperative.

Then I had him read the vision chart. His good eye read the chart perfectly.

"Okay, now cover your good eye and read the chart using your other eye."

He did as I instructed him, but didn't say anything.

After some silence, I asked, "What line can you read?"

"I can't see any of the lines."

He must have been mistaken. "Surely there must be at least one line you can read."

He squinted and shook his head. "No, I can't see anything."

I wrote down 'zero' on a piece of scrap paper and went to get our nurse. I explained to her what happened. She was a very caring and skilled nurse. She buzzed our ER doctor who came right out from the doctor's lounge. While he examined the boy's eye, the nurse told our receptionist she had to make a chart. I had gotten his name and date of birth, but that's all. No phone, no address. But the boy needed help. Who cared about a couple of blank lines on a chart?

Our ER doctor, an excellent physician, decided a specialist needed to see the patient. We called the eye-surgeon on top of our on-call list. He arrived within an hour.

The surgeon looked at the chart and then asked me, "What was the reading of his bad eye on the vision test?"

"Zero," I said.

The doctor looked startled. "Zero? He certainly must have seen something."

I shook my head. "No. Nothing."

"My God." He hurried into the room. After examining the patient, the surgeon called Phoenix Desert Hospital to schedule an operating room.

"How bad is his eye?" I asked the surgeon.

"He needs surgery. Right away. It's good he came in. If he had waited, even a few more hours, he'd have completely lost his eyesight in that eye."

This surgeon had a great reputation so we knew the young man would be in good hands. We called a cab for the patient to get to the hospital and gave him a pre-paid voucher from the hospital.

As he left, he smiled at all of us and said, "Thanks." Neither the doctor nor Phoenix Desert Hospital would make any money off that case, but we didn't care.

Thank God my curiosity had gotten the best of me and I rounded the corner to talk to him. I'm glad it was quiet that afternoon so he hadn't slipped out in the shuffle. I'm glad our wonderful nurse told the receptionist to check him into our computer system to produce a chart. I'm glad one of the best eye-surgeons in town helped him without any thought to payment.

And I'm glad we were able to help that young man. The thought of him going back to the field just a few feet away from us to live with that infected, painful eye, going blind in a few hours without any help, made me sick to my stomach.

Situations like this made all the stress of my job worthwhile. Loving my job and feeling useful helped me overlook the occasional rude person.

I still think of that young man every now and then after all these years, and I hope he isn't still homeless. He'd be in his forties by now. Today, I'm grateful he can walk by the building that once housed our facility and know the people in there years ago cared enough to save his sight.

***

One busy afternoon a young woman, early twenties, rushed through the doors into our emergency center holding a one-year-old in her arms. "Help! My baby, my baby! Somebody, please, help me!" She grasped her baby girl tightly in her arms and frantically looked around for someone to help her then ran over to the receptionist's desk, forcing her way ahead of the many other patients waiting their turn in the lobby.

While sitting in the nurse's station just a few feet away, I heard the hysteria in the young mother's voice and saw the panic in her face. I jumped up to help her and rushed her back to an empty bed. The girl paced up and down, refusing to let go of her baby. I learned later this was her only child.

"What happened?" I asked. The child's color looked pink and healthy-looking, not blue. I couldn't see anything wrong that jumped out at me but the mother's hysteria concerned me.

The young mother barely got the words out. "My baby! My baby!" was all she could say, hugging the child.

"Please, calm down and tell me what the problem is." Trying to hurry, I searched for a pen in my pocket and some paper to write down the vital signs until I had a chart.

"The paramedics," she said, her breaths coming in gasps. "The paramedics. They told me to bring her here."

"The paramedics were at your house?" Something terrible must have happened.

"Yes. I called 9-1-1."

She appeared to be calming down a little, so I pressed for more information. "And why did you call the paramedics?" I thought perhaps the baby had been choking. Or maybe a near drowning and had been treated. Near-drownings are common in our Valley of the Sun.

"She cut herself. With a scissors."

I couldn't see any blood and the little girl didn't appear in any distress. "Where?" I didn't see any blood anywhere.

"On her finger. Look! Here!" She held her daughter's wrist and thrust the girl's hand out for me to see.

I examined the tiny hand and fingers but couldn't see anything. Was I blind? "Where's the cut?"

The young mother glared at me in disbelief, like she could barely contain her anger. "It's right here. On her finger!" She screamed at me and pointed to the baby's ring finger.

I examined the finger but couldn't see anything except for a barely discernible, minute mark. "You mean this little paper cut?" I couldn't believe what I was, or wasn't, seeing.

She stared at me, her eyes narrowed and her mouth curled into a snarl. "IT WAS A SCISSORS!" She spat out the words, punctuating each one slowly.

The receptionist came back to the bedside to obtain information from the mother to generate a chart. Meanwhile, I cleaned the baby's finger using antiseptic soap and water. Then our patient emergency room doctor examined her and ordered antibiotic ointment and a band-aid®.

Getting a band-aid® onto that tiny finger was no easy feat. I wrapped it around as best as I could, but the child, who was well-behaved, wouldn't hold her hand still. And as soon as I finished, she popped the digit into her mouth.

I handed the mother the standard written follow-up instructions on wound care. "Keep it clean and dry. See your family doctor for any signs of infection."

The following week, a segment on a local news show dedicated to protecting consumers, "Three on Your Side", did a story on Phoenix Desert Hospital. "The $100 band-aid®." A reporter interviewed the young mother. "My baby cut her finger on a scissors and I took her to that emergency center. All they did was put a band-aid® on her finger, which came off by the time we got home. Then they sent us a bill for one hundred dollars."

One of our administrative doctors, who hadn't even been there that day, spoke to the reporter. He defended the hospital's fees, stating it was a minimum fee.

I wish the news station had bothered to interview me. I would have told them how this hysterical mother cut in front of other patients, for nothing more than an injury no larger than a paper cut. I would have let everyone know how she called the paramedics, took the time of the doctor, the receptionist, and myself, and occupied a bed while other patients who were truly ill waited.

But then, nobody asked me.

***

A chart lay on the counter. I picked it up. In the complaints section, the receptionist had typed, "Patient states he needs to see a doctor."

I brought the man back to a room. In his early forties, he was well-dressed in well-shined shoes, a business suit and tie. He removed his jacket and sat on the examining table.

"My wife and I separated for a while. We're back together now. But while we were separated, I picked up a hitchhiker and had sex with her. And now," he shifted uncomfortably and adjusted his tie, "now I seem to have symptoms of V.D."

"What are your symptoms?" I asked.

"Drainage. Pain. Burning."

I recorded this on the chart. "Okay, the doctor will be in shortly to see you. You'll need to undress and put on this gown." I handed him a sheet and gown and left the room.

When our doctor came out after examining the patient, he handed me two items: a glass slide of the man's genital discharge for me to gram stain and examine, and also a culturette of the discharge he had collected for a culture.

After donning gloves, I stained the slide and slipped it under the microscope lens to review. I saw lots of white cells and sure enough, many had gram negative diplococci bacteria in them—a sure sign of gonorrhea.

The doctor gave him a prescription for an antibiotic.

Two days later, I worked another twelve-hour shift. Once the patients started coming in, they never stopped. We couldn't get a break. By mid-afternoon, none of us had had lunch. The pile of patients' charts continued to grow higher and people packed the lobby. All we could do was just keep on trucking.

One after another, we brought back patients. When there was finally a room available, I brought back a woman whose chart only said, "Patient states she wants to see the doctor." She was about forty, nice looking and neatly dressed in business attire. She had combed her short brown hair into a neat hairstyle. When I finished taking her vital signs, I asked, "What seems to be the problem today?"

She fidgeted nervously and wrung her hands. "I want to be checked for V.D." she whispered.

"Do you have any symptoms?"

"No, but my husband was here a couple days ago and he has it, so I want to be checked." Panic covered her face. She was clearly upset. I looked at the name and then realized she was the wife of our previous patient who had gonorrhea.

"But you don't have any symptoms?" I repeated.

"No," she said then added, "and I don't want to be charged for this visit."

I looked at her, sure I had misheard her. I blinked my eyes. "Excuse me?"

"I work for my insurance company. I don't want them to know about this. It's too humiliating. I don't want to be charged for this visit. I just want a prescription."

Since when were we a free clinic? "The doctor will be with you in a while," I said. Let him decide what to do.

I brought the chart into the nurse's station and added it to the growing pile for the doctor to see. The receptionist walked back and added another chart to the pile of patients who needed to be placed in a room. "There are more waiting to be checked in," she said. They would just have to wait until a room opened.

The doctor, nurse, x-ray tech and I looked at each other and sighed. "It'll be a long wait before we get lunch," someone said. We were all hungry and tired. We were so busy we couldn't even eat in shifts. Somebody told a quick joke to relieve the tension and we all laughed. We needed that relief, if even just for a moment.

Eventually our doctor asked, "Who's in the GYN room?"

"It's the wife of a patient we had a couple days ago," I said. "He's being treated for gonorrhea. She doesn't have symptoms but wants a prescription. She's freaked."

He nodded and picked up the chart.

"By the way," I added, "she doesn't want to be charged."

The nurse and doctor looked at each other. "So we're a welfare clinic now?" the nurse asked.

The doctor went back to the GYN room, but returned in a moment. "There's no one in there. Where did she go?"

I shrugged my shoulders. "Maybe the bathroom. I'm sure she'll be back." We were too busy to go looking for her. The doctor simply grabbed another chart and went to a different patient in another room.

A few minutes later, our receptionist brought back another chart and handed it to me. Then she walked three feet to the med room where our nurse was getting medication for a patient.

The receptionist asked our nurse. "Why is Karen in the lobby giving a patient the name and phone number of the hospital president and telling her to call him?" Karen was our x-ray tech that day.

"What?" our nurse asked, too busy to think of a patient in the lobby.

"Yeah. Karen is urging the woman to call the hospital's CEO. I heard her spelling out the doctor's name and the rest of your names."

Our nurse looked at the receptionist in disbelief then looked at me. "Do you know what's going on with Karen?"

"No. Nothing. I've been busy."

Our nurse replaced the medication, relocked the drawer, and

ran out to the lobby.

I went out to the lobby to get the next patient. Right beside the door sat the woman who wanted to be treated free of charge, sobbing hysterically. I saw Karen sitting next to her, smiling and beaming, as if proud of herself. *What was going on?*

Our nurse sat down next to the sobbing woman. "Can I help you?"

The woman blew her nose. "You're all laughing at me. I heard you laughing. All of you. Even the doctor. I just wanted to be checked because my husband," she looked around and dropped her voice, "has V.D. He was here a couple days ago. And you're all laughing at me."

"Oh, ma'am, we're not laughing at you. It's just a very busy day today," our nurse said. "We're all under a lot of tension. Someone told a joke and we laughed. It had nothing to do with you. Really."

"This other woman I was just talking to," she pointed to Karen sitting on the other side of her, "told me to call the president of Phoenix Desert Hospital and complain. She gave me all your names."

Karen sat up straight, lifted her chin, beamed with pride, and pressed her thin lips into a huge smile.

"Well, ma'am, there's no need for that. I'm sure we can settle this," our nurse said in a soothing voice.

"And my insurance company can't be charged for this. I've been seen at this hospital before and my insurance information is in their records. But I work there and I don't want anyone at work to know about this. So I can't be charged."

I wished I could have wiped the smug look off Karen's face but I didn't have the time. I took the next patient back.

Our tactful nurse somehow calmed the hysterical patient down and got her to return to the exam room. Our doctor talked with her, wrote a prescription, then drew a big X across his billing sheet and wrote NC—No Charge. Our nurse did the same to our billing sheet. We didn't want our hospital president to receive any complaints about our center, even though he probably would have made her pay since we weren't a free clinic.

The patient left happy and evidently never called the president of Phoenix Desert Hospital to complain about us because we didn't hear anything. She was one satisfied customer—a satisfied, free-of-charge, customer.

I don't know why Karen tried to get us all into trouble. She was usually a nice person. Some people get satisfaction out of creating controversy for their co-workers, I guess. Maybe they think it makes them look good, by comparison. Maybe they see their co-workers as competition instead of part of a team working together. Maybe they don't understand the concept of teamwork.

In the interest of getting along at work, I knew I had to get over it, forgive and repay with kindness. I hated petty feuds at work.

***

For many years, playing tennis topped my list of things I wanted to learn. My daughter frequently spent time with her friends now, leaving me home alone. So I decided to take lessons and join a tennis club.

As a beginner player, I met a few ladies my age but because all the male beginner players were over eighty years old, I wasn't meeting men my age. But what the heck, I was having fun, gaining female friends, getting some exercise and working my way up the ranks.

I even gathered up the nerve to attend a summer social tennis party at the group leader's house. No one I knew planned to be there. I've never liked going places alone, so I felt pretty nervous. I told myself I would go to the party and stay for just thirty minutes. If I wasn't having any fun, I could drive home and finish the mystery I was reading. Thirty minutes—I could handle that. Plus a good book. Not a bad Friday night. I've had worse.

Amy was staying overnight at her best friend's house so I forced myself to drive to the party. Taking a deep breath, I knocked on the door, walked into a crowd of strangers, checked my watch—eight p.m.—took a glass of wine cooler and meandered out to the patio. Finding the food table, I proceeded to fill up a plate of snacks and decided to hang out at the snack table for a while. But everyone seemed to know everyone else and formed little groups, making me feel out of place.

Imagining that I didn't belong and feeling very much alone, I found an empty chair and sat down, keeping myself busy munching on snacks as I watched the other party-goers. A bite of chips and salsa. A sip of wine cooler. More chips and salsa. Another sip of wine. Smile at passerby. Another bite of chips and salsa. Eight twenty-five. I didn't know what to do with myself. Why was it men could go somewhere alone and not feel awkward? Looking around, I mentally mapped a surreptitious exit. My mystery book beckoned to me.

Suddenly, a man sat down in the chair next to me. "Hi, my name is Mike. Are you new in the club?"

Startled by someone actually paying attention to me, I froze. I'm sure my eyes popped wide open as I stared at him. Cute! Sweet! Friendly! Quickly swallowing the wad of food crammed in my mouth, I managed to mumble, "Um, yeah, I just joined."

He stayed and talked. His amiable voice and gentle manner captivated me. He radiated sweetness and he spoke intelligently. I could have listened to him all night yet he showed interest in what I had to say. I sensed nothing phony about him, just pure friendliness. He didn't try to hit on me, yet he didn't hide that he found me attractive enough to sit and talk to for a portion of the evening. He couldn't stop smiling at me, even his soft blue eyes radiated warmth. I instantly felt comfortable around him, as if I'd known him for a long time.

Suddenly he looked around. "I have to go now. Nice meeting you." Then he got up and left—with another woman! That's it? My heart sank as I watched him walk out the door with a nice-looking petite blonde lady. He hadn't even asked me for my phone number, or suggested we get together, or anything.

Disappointed, I waited for them to leave so I could depart myself. Just as I popped another chip into my mouth, another man sat down in his place. We'll call him Francis. Francis was not cute and he had bad breath. Francis did not seem friendly, or sweet, or nice. He kind of leered at me and I couldn't get rid of him. On and on and on he talked until I finally could excuse myself and slip away, out to my car, back home to safety. To safety and security and Agatha Christie.

I called Liz in Hawaii and told her all about my evening. "Typical. The cute, nice ones end up with someone else. And the ones interested in me are the ones I don't want!"

"Keep trying. Something good will happen eventually," she assured me. She always gave good advice.

But this time I wasn't so sure.

I joined a women's tennis team. We played at various beautiful resorts all over the valley—The Wigwam in Litchfield, The Pointe-Tapatio in central Phoenix, various resorts in Scottsdale. We had a great time, helped me deal with the stress of work, and gave me experience on the courts. I got to know some fun ladies with whom I occasionally socialized. We'd play tennis together socially and go to happy hours.

Growing up in Minnesota, I ate home-style country cooking—meat and potatoes. In Hawaii, Asian food dominated my taste buds. Now in Arizona, Mexican restaurants surrounded me. Salsa became my condiment of choice. At the happy hours I had chips, salsa and tacitos alongside a margarita in a glass rimmed with salt. Mexican restaurants had a feeling of gaiety about them, with music playing and plenty of food, always providing a great time. I had fun going to happy hours with friends.

Over the next few months, I looked for Mike every time I went to the tennis courts but never saw him. The advanced players played different evenings than the beginners.

Three months later, the morning after Thanksgiving, my daughter went to a friend's house and I had the day off of work. I was sitting at home drinking a cup of coffee when the phone rang. It was Jane, a new acquaintance of mine from my tennis group. "My boyfriend just called me," she said. "He has a friend who wants to play mixed doubles tennis this afternoon and we need a fourth. Are you available?"

Fortunately, I had the afternoon free. We arranged to meet at the Scottsdale Community College tennis courts at two p.m. Since I lived on the other side of town, I had the farthest to drive so naturally I got there first. I had never met Jane's boyfriend before, I barely knew her, but I hoped whoever he was that he had an attractive, sweet friend for me. Sure would be nice.

A car pulled up. Jane got out. We sat on a bench talking, waiting for the guys when another car pulled up in the parking lot. I couldn't believe my eyes!

It was Mike.

Gasping, I turned to Jane and blurted, "Jane, do you

remember me mentioning to you about a party last August where I met a really nice guy I really liked and we talked for a long time but then he left with some blonde?"

"Yes." She nodded her head, swinging her dark brunette hair.

"Well, that's him!"

He got out of the car and walked toward us.

She looked down at me, her face suddenly locked in a look of superiority and cooed, "That's my boyfriend."

Huh? My body went numb and I stared at her, my eyes suddenly unable to blink. Things couldn't have gotten much worse.

Before I recovered from the shock, another car drove up and out stepped Francis, the man I had escaped from at the summer social. My date for the day.

Yup, things had gotten worse.

I was the weakest player of the foursome and Francis and I were losing. I kept hitting the ball into the net, making Francis angry. Or I hit the ball long, upsetting Francis. Apparently, Francis didn't like losing. Over and over he gave me dirty looks and shook his head in disbelief at my lack of ability. And when Jane looked at me, the look on her face gloated.

By contrast, Mike acted sweet and encouraging, giving me advice. "It would help if you hit the ball crosscourt." Or, "When you volley, just punch the ball, like this."

I smiled my gratitude, forcing back the tears, relieved at least one person acted amicably toward me. He was five feet ten, a skilled player, and cute. Stop noticing! I had to get him out of my head. He belonged to Jane.

Somehow I got through that nightmare of a day. Over the next few months, Jane would call me to say things like, "Mike and I went to the movies last night," or, "Mike and I are going to a Tina Turner concert this weekend." So I moved on and lived my own life, improving in tennis, moving up the ranks and meeting other men but nothing clicked for me.

I took tennis lessons, playing three to four times a week. My skills improved so much, I moved up into the same group as Mike's. The joy tingling through me at the sight of him again surprised me. Then I heard through the grapevine that he wasn't seeing Jane anymore. She had moved to the other side of the valley and didn't play in our club anymore, so we probably wouldn't run into each other.

I gave Mike a huge smile.

He returned a smile and said, "Maybe we could get together sometime and play tennis?"

Yahoo! A couple weeks later, he called and we went out and hit some balls around the court. Afterwards we grabbed a bite to eat.

Conversation flowed easily. We learned we had been born three days and sixty miles apart from each other in Minnesota, meeting forty years later in a little tennis group in Phoenix. Coincidence, or was it fate? His family had moved to Phoenix when he turned seven. He had five siblings, just like me. He came from a working-class family, just like mine. We held the same political and religious views. Not only did I feel at ease around him, but I was definitely attracted to him.

I came to realize he was a little shy. He liked to become friends with a woman first before getting into a heavy relationship. That was great by me because I also liked to take things slow. Over the next few months we went to movies, to the symphony, played tennis, ate pizza, had fun, and got to know each other. I began to think of him as my soul mate. He was friendly to Amy and she heartily approved of him. I looked forward to discovering where our friendship would lead.

***

I told Mike about my work, including one of my favorite emergency doctors—Dr. H. She was friendly, cared about the patients, and things moved swiftly when she worked. A couple of times, she and some of the emergency center staff met at a restaurant for lunch when off-duty. I enjoyed those days.

Her latest project involved producing a children's safety video. One hot summer Saturday afternoon, she walked through our freestanding emergency center door, followed by an entourage of people I had never seen before. A pretty nurse from Phoenix Desert Hospital, a couple paramedics, a ten-year-old boy who was the star of the video, a director who was probably in his thirties and his crew, all filed in. They set up equipment to film the video in a back room of our little center.

The video's story centered around the boy/actor who pretended to fall while riding his bicycle in the desert. The video would teach children safety precautions and what to expect if they ever had to go to an emergency room.

The boy/actor lay on a bed, a cervical collar around his neck. They needed someone to be the receptionist for the film. I was on duty and Dr. H. roped me into doing it. She was a sweetie and I would've done anything for her, although being in the video didn't excite me.

Up front, actual sick patients checked in nonstop. I ran back and forth between the front of the center helping my co-workers, and the pretend ER filming in the back room. Our real nurse and x-ray tech had to pick up the slack with our patients since I couldn't help them very much. I felt bad but they were just glad they didn't have to be in the film themselves.

The film director, a young cocky guy who walked around like he was a Hollywood big shot, barked orders to his crew. His nose pointed in the air. He walked our halls as if he managed the entire center, forgetting he was our guest for the day.

He said to me, "You need to walk over to the bed and say, 'I have to put this on your wrist.' Then put this ID bracelet on the boy while the doctor and nurse examine him. That's all you gotta do. Then walk out. Do you think you can handle that?" His tone oozed condescension.

Gee whiz. Yes, I think I can handle that. What a condescending hot dog! I didn't like his tone and attitude but was already committed to the project.

Dr. H. had received permission from Phoenix Desert Hospital for filming. Our doctor on duty at our center that day also said it was okay to film and agreed to volunteer me for the project.

I didn't want to go on-camera wearing my glasses. I was young and insecure. Without my glasses on, I couldn't see well enough to clasp the boy/actor's ID bracelet. To solve the problem, I clasped the bracelet together first, held it in my hands then took off my glasses and waited in the wings until I heard my cue.

My cue! I entered the room. "I have to put this on your wrist." I lifted the boy's hand, slipped on the ID band I had already clasped together, and walked out.

Whew. Not so bad. Cinch!

The hot-dog director marched over to me, pointed to the camera and snipped in a sarcastic voice, "Do you see that?"

I nodded.

"That's called a camera." He pronounced the word using three slow syllables, like I didn't have a brain in my head.

Yes, I know what that's called. I nodded.

"You can't stand in front of the camera, blocking everyone else." He glared at me, obviously thinking he was way superior to me.

Oh. Guess I went to school to be a Med Tech, not an actress, Buddy. Back out to the wings. Glasses back on. Clasped a new ID bracelet together in a circle. Glasses off again. Heard my cue. Entered the room. Didn't block the camera. "I have to put this on your wrist." Lifted boy's hand. Slipped on ID bracelet over wrist. Walked out. Perfect!

After I finished acting the receptionist in the film, I zipped to the front of our center to help my co-workers who were swamped. One of our patients was a twelve-year-old girl experiencing LRQ—lower right quadrant—abdominal pain. This is a symptom of appendicitis, a life-threatening condition if not treated properly and promptly. Our ER doctor on duty at the time ordered blood work on the patient.

I drew the little girl's blood and analyzed it. I prepared a blood slide and set it aside to dry so I could stain it for microscopic examination.

A film crewmember popped his head into my lab. "Sorry, we have to shoot that scene again. The doctor omitted one of her lines." At least this guy spoke politely.

After a huge sigh, I ran to the rear of the center and repeated the process. Glasses on. Clasped another ID bracelet. Glasses off. Waited for cue, etc., this time thinking only of my possible appendicitis patient and hoping the filming would go fast.

Finished the scene. Good. The blood slide should be dry by now and I can finish the test. I returned to the lab. Grabbing the stains, I went through the staining procedure. Just as I sat down at the microscope, the video-director poked his head into the lab again, telling me I needed to return to the shooting of the scene.

What now?

The director said, "It's been called to our attention you are lifting the boy's hand off the bed to slip the ID band onto his wrist." He shot me an angry look. I resented his attitude, mainly because I was a volunteer. I didn't get paid to take his bad attitude.

"That's right." *Hurry it up, Hot-Dog, I have work to do.*

"Well, the doctor said you can't do that. It's supposed to be a neck injury. You can't lift his hand. You have to slip the bracelet under his wrist and then clasp it," he said through clenched teeth. His lip raised in a sneer. He rolled his eyes at me and shook his head.

I nodded. *Let's just get this over with.* I forced myself to return, my pace slowing with each step. New ID bracelet. Took off my glasses. Waited in wings for cue. Entered room. Didn't block camera. "I have to put this on your wrist." Slipped bracelet under his wrist and tried to clasp it together.

Oh, no!! Without my glasses on, I couldn't see well enough to clasp it together. I tried and tried and tried.

Couldn't get the blasted thing to stay together.

"CUT!" The director's anger looked as if it might erupt any second. He marched over to where I stood and towered over me. "What's wrong now?"

"I can't see without my glasses."

Huge sigh from Mr. Hot-Dog director. "Well-maybe-you-could-put-your-glasses-on?" He spoke in a slow, patronizing tone, as if speaking to a one-year-old.

I wanted to punch him right in the middle of his patronizing face. Hey, I'm only asking one measly little thing. "I don't want to go on camera wearing glasses." I refused to back down to this guy. He acted as if I worked for him, forgetting I was simply doing them a favor and really didn't want to do this at all.

Dr. H. showed her gratitude for doing this favor. "Let's take a break for a few minutes," she said, in an attempt to defuse the situation.

Good! I ran to the lab, finished my microscopic analysis of the patient's blood, and turned in the results. My patient had a high white count, indicating appendicitis. We transferred her to the hospital for immediate surgery.

I then had a few minutes available, so I grabbed a handful of ID bracelets and practiced clasping them together without wearing my glasses. I finally could do it and we re-shot the segment. I was sweating in the heat and very nervous. The outside temperature hit one hundred-fifteen degrees in the shade that afternoon. The many large lights required for filming caused the heat in our center to rise higher than usual.

But I did it. Success! Yeah! Thank God I finally finished my segment of the film. But the video wasn't done. They had to film more scenes but my presence wasn't required. The crew continued to film, their intense lights heating the rooms even more. The heat emanated throughout the center and our old A/C gave us all it had.

I went to the refrigerator in our lounge to get a cold soda. When I opened the fridge door, a blue light shot across the interior in the shape of an arc. My breathing stopped for a moment while I stared at the scary sight. Quickly recognizing the danger, I slammed the door shut.

Running down the hallway, I saw a group of people standing outside the x-ray room. They were filming the actor/boy being x-rayed, while a paramedic pretended to be an x-ray tech. One of the guys standing in the hallway had a stocky build, with bulging biceps looking as solid as steel. Probably a paramedic, I reasoned. I needed not only his muscles but also a paramedic's training with electrical emergencies. "Are you a paramedic?"

He nodded.

There wasn't time to explain. "Come. Quick!"

My face must have reflected the frantic fear I felt inside because without any question, he immediately followed me as I rushed to the lounge.

I pointed to the fridge. "When I opened the door, a beam of blue light arced across the inside."

He immediately jumped into action. "Stand back," he ordered, grabbing my shoulders and pushing me aside. He retrieved special gloves/paraphernalia then heaved the heavy refrigerator away from the wall and unplugged it.

My hero! It must've been the combination of the Phoenix summer heat beating through the windows plus all the film equipment and hot lights on top of our usual electrical usage that stressed the system, causing a potentially dangerous electrical hazard to anyone touching the refrigerator.

Air conditioners struggle to cool buildings down in Phoenix because it gets so hot here in the summertime. The A/C wasn't the only thing stressed by the heat. After an entire day of being strapped on a bed, a cervical collar wrapped around his neck, bright lights shining straight down on him and a barely functioning A/C, the little boy/actor got sick and vomited repeatedly in the bathroom, his skin drained of all color. This worried me but his father was a paramedic and took good care of him.

The whole film crew left at the end of the day, leaving their mess behind them. The actor/boy's father took him home. Our actual nurse worked on more patients. Our real x-ray tech and I cleaned up after the film crew and returned everything to its rightful place. I guess Mr. Hot Dog director thought we had nothing else to do but clean up after him and his crew.

Because this happened on a Saturday, it took three days for Phoenix Desert Hospital to order and replace our refrigerator. Administration doesn't work on weekends. In the meantime, someone at the main hospital sent out coolers full of ice. The hottest days of the year, and we lived out of coolers of ice which began to melt halfway through the long days. It was miserable.

But I got a free copy of the safety video and now I show it to my grandchildren. And I smile as I see myself slipping the ID bracelet on the boy's wrist, not blocking a soul, and reciting my big line, "I have to put this on your wrist."

And I fantasize about glaring at Mr. Hot-Dog director, then pointing outside the door towards our real emergency room up front and saying, "See that? That's called a real job." And then, in my fantasy, he apologizes profusely for being so rude to me. And I feel better.

***

After I had worked at the emergency centers for a couple years, a mother brought in her ten-year-old daughter. "She has to go to the bathroom a lot, and often seems tired. I thought maybe she might have a bladder infection or something," the mother said.

I took the girl's vital signs, then showed them the restroom and told the mother to collect a urine sample using the kit I handed her. When I started walking back to the nursing station to wait for them to finish, the mother made an offhand remark, "You know, she seems to be thirsty all the time."

117

I stopped in my tracks and turned around. "What did you say?"

The mother looked worried. "She seems to be thirsty all the time. Just lately. I didn't know if that was important or not." She closed the bathroom door.

You bet it's important! I wrote the mother's remark on the chart, circling it in red.

Most days we were only moderately busy. Occasionally we were very slow and occasionally we were very busy. Fortunately we had been fairly slow that particular day so we could give our full attention to the little girl.

Our doctor ordered blood work on the child—CBC— Complete Blood Count of the cells, and glucose—the blood sugar. Suspecting the girl had diabetes, I immediately diluted the serum by two after spinning the blood in the centrifuge. The result was still out of range! I then diluted it by three and also by four, and ran both samples. Finally I got a reading and was able to multiply, getting over eleven hundred. This was eleven times over the normal value of one hundred.

A glucose level that high, along with her symptoms, indicated juvenile diabetes. I felt bad for the girl but her mother impressed me as being level-headed and responsible so the child would be well taken care of. I handed my written report to the doctor waiting in the nurse's station.

Our doctor took one look at the incredibly high result and turned to our male receptionist sitting next to him. "Call Phoenix Desert Hospital and tell them we need a room for her."

I pulled up a stool and sat down next to the doctor and receptionist behind the glass window in the nurse's station.

The receptionist picked up the phone and called the admitting department at the hospital across town. "This is the emergency center calling. We need to admit a patient." He listened for a while then a few seconds later said, "Okay" and hung up. He turned to our doctor and said, "They're not admitting any patients right now. There's-"

"What do you mean they're not taking any patients?" our doctor bellowed. "I happen to know there are plenty of beds available. You call them back and tell them they will give that girl a room."

"You didn't let me finish," the receptionist said, his voice calm and steady. "There's a gunman in the house. They're not letting anybody in."

A gunman in the hospital? I covered my mouth to cover my gasp. I shuddered as I thought about those poor employees over there responsible for all the helpless patients while a gunman ran around loose. I wondered if anyone I knew was working right then.

The doctor shook his head. "I don't care. This girl needs to be in a hospital. You call them back and tell them they're taking this patient."

Our receptionist didn't make a move. Instead, he clenched his teeth, lowered his voice and spoke slowly, enunciating each word. "I'm not going to send a child over to the hospital while a gunman is there!" He stared at the doctor, almost daring him to challenge.

The doctor blinked, as if understanding the situation for the first time. I knew that particular doctor well enough to know he was a very caring, intelligent person and excellent doctor. I would've trusted him with my family's lives. Maybe physicians are so used to having everyone jump at their commands, they don't stop and think things through. It takes a while for them to listen to what someone else is saying. They only react to not being instantly obeyed. Getting medical care for his patient dominated his first thoughts, blinding him to everything else happening around him. I knew he'd take the best action for the little girl once he thought about it.

"Oh. Okay. Well, call Children's Hospital and get her in there."

The nurse did the necessary transfer paperwork and sent the girl and her mother to Children's Hospital.

Later in the evening, we learned what had happened at Phoenix Desert Hospital. A boy in his twenties lay unconscious in ICU. Waving a gun, the patient's brother had burst onto the floor and held everyone hostage, threatening to kill the staff if his brother died. The hospital went into lockdown mode. Police swarmed the grounds. The ICU doctor talked the boy into surrendering and the police arrested him.

Then our phone rang. I answered. The voice of a young-sounding man identified himself as the doctor down at Children's Hospital. "I just wanted to know how much insulin you gave this patient," he asked.

I turned to the nurse. "Children's wants to know how much insulin you gave to the girl."

"I didn't give her any insulin."

I turned back to the phone. "She didn't get any insulin," I related to the doctor.

"Our lab here ran a glucose and it's seven hundred. I wanted to know how much insulin she got."

"Well, we didn't give her any. We sent her immediately to you."

The young doctor sighed and said, "Okay" and hung up.

Yikes! I had gotten over four hundred milligrams percent more than they did! Were my readings off? Or my dilutions? I couldn't get it out of my mind and had to know. If I had made a mistake, it would've caused me to question my skills forever. So for my own peace of mind, I called a taxi and sent the specimen to our main lab at Phoenix Desert Hospital to be re-run. I didn't alert the hospital lab tech about my result. I wanted to see what she would get.

Our main lab's chemistry department eventually called to tell me her result. She got almost exactly what I had—less than zero point two milligrams percent different than my result.

Whew! Two lab techs, two separate methods, and results that close. That was excellent. Glad my result had been correct, I realized the girl must still have been producing a little bit of insulin. Relieved, I was able to get a good night's sleep after crawling into bed. If I had been wrong, I knew sleep would have evaded me all night. I was pretty sure nearly everyone in the medical field felt the same way I did. We could do nine hundred and ninety-nine things exactly right, even performing miracles, but if we did one thing wrong it haunted us because it could mean disaster for the patient.

Doctors, nurses, lab, x-ray, therapists, all of us worked together as a team and if one person made a mistake, we all suffered. The possibility of a mistake reminded us why we needed to help each other—for the sake of the patient. At the emergency center, we usually helped each other and consequently, we had a lot of success stories, like this little girl who got the medical attention she needed.

Most days, we had a slow but steady stream of patients at the emergency center. Sometimes we were very slow. And there were occasional days when we were so busy, we didn't even have time to go to the bathroom.

At first, our centers were open twenty-four hours a day. But economic considerations required us to reduce our hours. My shift changed to 11:00 a.m. to 11:00 p.m. If the doctor ordered any lab tests, I was on stand-by from 7:00 a.m. to 11:00 a.m. Amy was old enough now to be home alone in the mornings if I got called in before she went to school. After school and on weekends when I worked, she went to a friend's place or my parents'. I loved having seven days off every other week.

One work-morning I was sound asleep at eight o'clock when the phone rang, jarring me awake and out of a sweet dream. "We need you for some lab work," our nurse at the emergency center said.

I made good money being on stand-by, and the crew on duty that day was fun to work with, so I gladly hopped out of bed, brushed my teeth, slapped on some make-up, threw on a top and some white pants, pulled on my white nursing shoes, and dashed out the door, zipping to the emergency center in my little blue Plymouth Sundance, arriving by 8:30 a.m.

The doctor had ordered a slew of tests. My machines had been soaking overnight so I got them running, ran controls, and organized things for the day. Our efficient nurse had drawn the blood for me.

By the time I finished analyzing all the ordered tests, another patient had checked in who needed lab. Thus began a non-stop stream of patients, one sick patient after another after another. We barely kept up. It seemed everybody needed CBC's, electrolytes, cardiac enzymes, liver profiles, blood sugar levels, kidney tests, urine tests, or the occasional blood gas.

Our lab didn't possess the most sophisticated equipment in the history of the world and I had to run each test individually, so it took a while to complete everything. As soon as I finished working on one patient, the doctor ordered more tests on the next patient.

Our x-ray tech was swamped taking x-rays and our nurse handled all the other patients by herself.

Around noon, one of our patients required a gram stain and culture. We sent all cultures to the main lab at Phoenix Desert Hospital, but I was supposed to read the gram stains first before sending them on to the main lab for a final "official" reading by the microbiology lab techs. Our doctor told me, "I don't need an initial reading of the gram stain. I'm letting this patient go with a prescription. Just send the stain over to the hospital to be read later."

Whew! I had enough to do.

Requisition slips piled up and the patients kept on coming. By two o'clock in the afternoon, the effects of hunger hit me. I hadn't had anything to eat all day, not even coffee to drink. Food and drink weren't allowed in a lab for health reasons. The receptionist, busy checking in another patient as I finished with another, called out, "Line Two—call for lab."

I didn't have time for phone calls! Squelching my irritation, I picked up the receiver and forced my voice to sound pleasant. "Laboratory, may I help you?"

"I just received a gram stain from you." The sound of our microbiology senior lab tech's frosty voice came across the phone. She was usually very friendly but not today. "Will you please explain to me why you didn't read it first?"

I held the phone to my ear and considered my reply. The receptionist's printer chugged out another chart across the hall. The front door opened with its tell-tale chime and in walked another patient. The lobby hummed with the chatter of more patients waiting to be brought to a room. The phone rang on the other line, blaring through the air again and again until someone had time to answer it. The x-ray tech called out a patient's name to take to our last available room. The nurse, running around frantic to get medications to all her patients, called out, "More lab tests ordered in Room Three."

My stomach growled. I could almost hear my stomach talking. I want breakfast! I want lunch! I want coffee!

Microbiology does not deal with "stats" other than gram stains from the ER. I'm not saying they're not busy in their department, but they work at their own pace and don't have to deal with emergencies. Cultures take their time growing. From experience, I knew she had had all her coffee and lunch breaks that day. Even though she worked as a department supervisor, I felt myself losing the grip on my temper.

Must've been my stomach talking. My blood sugar was surely low. My hands shook from hunger. And I practically would have killed for a cup of coffee. Her assumption that I had all the time in the world to read that stupid gram stain ticked me off.

I snapped, "They called me in at eight o'clock this morning. I haven't had any coffee yet today. I haven't had breakfast. I haven't had lunch. I've had to go to the bathroom for two hours. And it doesn't look like there's any end in sight. The doctor told me he didn't need a reading on the patient's slide. Now, if you don't mind, I'm swamped with work and I don't have time for this phone call."

She stammered, "Okay."

I could tell she was stunned at my response and tone of voice. Good. I hung up.

I felt awful because I really liked her, but I was too busy and too hungry to talk to someone who assumed I was sitting around on my butt too lazy to read a gram stain!

We eventually took turns for a couple minutes to shovel some food down our throats. We locked the doors at eleven p.m. so no one else could come in while we finished up, but still didn't get out of there that night until midnight. Because we had occasional slow days at the center, it actually felt good to work hard once in a while. It made me feel like our work made the world a better place since we had helped many people and done a good job. The nurse helped me. I helped her. When X-ray was busy and I had no lab, I went into X-ray and helped load films and develop the pictures. X-ray also helped the nurse and me. The receptionist was efficient and pleasant and hard-working. We had all worked together like a team.

Now I just needed to get the main lab at the main hospital to think of me as part of their team.

***

I kept playing tennis, getting good exercise. Mike asked me to be his partner in a weekend tournament. If we took first place, he would move up to the next level in the club, from the C's to the B's. I knew he badly wanted to advance and I felt honored he thought my skills were good enough to help him win. I really wanted to do my best for him.

To my horror, I played off the mark that day. By that time, I was experienced enough that I was pretty strong at the net. But that day I kept volleying into the net or sending it long. Our opponents returned as many balls to me as they could to keep the ball away from Mike. I felt terrible for ruining Mike's chances of moving up. He was counting on me.

I could barely face him. "I'm just going to let the ball go past me when I'm at the net, so you can hit it. I'm just ruining things for you." I choked back the tears. I figured he'd be relieved, since I was solely responsible for our having lost the first set and now we were down two to three in the second set. If we lost just three more quick games, we were out of the entire tournament and would go home as losers, and all because of me. I wanted to hide somewhere and never be seen on a court again.

Instead, he looked horrified, as if I had just told him his car had blown up. Grabbing hold of my shoulders, he said, "No! We'll never win that way. You've got to keep trying. You can do it." He gave me an encouraging smile, letting me know he still had faith in my ability.

I'd been playing tennis long enough to have witnessed many men getting upset at a female partner not playing well. But not Mike. He only got upset at himself.

I gave myself a little pep talk in my mind. I just needed to get over my nervousness and start to focus. Focus. Focus! I forced myself to think of the ball and nothing but the ball.

Mike served. The female opponent returned the ball. I stepped up to the net and slammed a volley.

It went in! A winner.

Mike served again. Our male opponent, a big man, returned it straight at my face, hard. Some male players liked to intimidate women. Our competitor obviously didn't know who he was dealing with. I refused to back away from the net.

I closed my eyes, ducked, and held up my racquet to protect my face.

It went in! A winner. The guy looked as shocked as I felt.

Thirty-love, our favor. Mike served again. Once more, I volleyed a winner.

Forty-love.

Mike served to the man next. Revealing a determined look on his face, the opponent reared back, stepped into it, and whipped a forehand as hard as he could. Right towards me.

Into the net.

I hid a smile as the ball rolled down the net on the opponent's side of the court. Our game! Now it was three to three in the second set. I continued to play the net, we continued to win and took the second set, six to four.

After our opponent's easy win the first set, I knew they felt they deserved to win the entire match. Their frustration grew and they began to rush things. They started making mistakes.

By contrast, I gained confidence and began playing better. Mike remained steady. We took the third set, winning the match.

We moved up the tournament ladder to the next match against new opponents, and beat them also. We returned the next day and won the tournament—First Place. We gladly took our hard -won trophies. Mike would move up to the B's in next month's tournament.

I still played in the C's and would miss him but felt happy for him. After the tournament, we joined other tennis players at the Elephant Bar and had burgers and beer.

Eventually I also moved up to the B's in our weekend club. We continued playing as partners in the Choose Your Own Partner tournaments.

Our friendship grew over time, including a mutual attraction and caring about each other. We made sure we saw each other twice a week and talked every day. Our social lives together consisted of tennis, movies, dinner, day trips around Arizona, the symphony, tennis parties, etc. We talked about everything.

I met his family and he met mine. He went to my parents' place for family dinners. My Dad liked him. They talked about and watched sports together. My mother adored him.

I hoped he wouldn't disappoint me like some other men had in the past. Trusting men presented a problem for me. The whole relationship thing scared me because I felt Mike slowly taking possession of my heart.

***

The hospital that owned us actually owned three emergency centers. I rotated through all three at various times. Just before Christmas one year, a friendly man brought his ten-year-old son into the Paradise Valley emergency center. The boy had a deep cut in his hand. We had to call in a hand-specialist to repair the injury.

The specialist swept in, barking orders. We took turns and this time I was the lucky one who got to assist the not-so-pleasant surgeon. He had a reputation as an excellent hand surgeon. I knew the patient would be in skilled hands, even though I didn't care for the doctor's personality.

I donned sterile gloves, opened the sterile tray, laid out the sterile instruments, poured betadine cleanser into its prescribed cup, and filled the sterile basin with saline for rinsing. All things I had performed multiple times before.

The boy's father sat on a stool next to the bed as the visiting hand-specialist surgeon began work on the patient. All other beds were vacant. The boy acted well-behaved and cooperated. I adjusted the overhead light to shine a spotlight on the injured hand.

"I need a bucket," the doctor said to me after a while.

A bucket? What an odd request. I had assisted many doctors who were suturing before and had never had a request for a bucket. Perhaps the boy had mentioned he felt nauseous, I thought. We used buckets to mix plaster in for splints but they could also be used for patients to vomit into.

The hand-specialist had an angry demeanor, so I didn't dare question him. The buckets, made of a cardboard type of material with a wax-like coating, were stacked high in the supply room. I went to retrieve one before the surgeon had time to complain.

When I returned to the bedside carrying the bucket, the doctor's gloved hands froze in midair. He glared at me, his eyes blinking repeatedly. His jaw dropped slightly before he finally said in an icy tone, "What is that?"

"It's a bucket." I gulped.

He growled, "I wanted a basin. A sterile basin for extra saline!"

Well, if you wanted a basin you should have asked for a

126

basin. But you asked for a bucket! I forced a weak smile. "Oh. Okay. I'll get a basin." I quickly brought a sterile basin, unwrapped it and poured saline into it.

"And I need more betadine."

I squeezed the plastic betadine bottle, squirting the brown soapy solution into the cup.

Horrified, the doctor barked, "Higher!"

Startled, I raised the bottle, then squirted a stream of betadine into the cup.

"Lower!" he shouted.

What? Getting nervous now, I lowered the bottle, betadine still streaming out.

My actions made him even angrier, if that was possible. "Higher!"

I held my breath. I didn't know what to do. Nothing I did satisfied him. Once again I raised the bottle.

Holding his gloved hands in the air like he was singing 'Hallelujah', he jumped off his stool and stormed into the dirty laundry room where we kept instruments that needed cleaning, the closest private room available. "Come with me," he shouted behind him.

Terrified by now, I happened to glance at the patient's father. He looked furious. "What's wrong with that guy?" the father asked me. He got up and started pacing the floor.

I shrugged my shoulders and scurried after the doctor. No time for questions. When I entered the laundry room, the doctor whirled around to face me and snarled, "WHAT IS YOUR NAME?"

Thank God my badge wasn't on my lab coat right then. I felt like I floated above, watching the scene below me. Too scared to think straight, I heard a far-off quivering voice sounding strangely a lot like mine. It said, "My name is Martha."

Martha was one of our nurses. Okay, so that was a horrible thing for me to do. But fear makes people do odd things. Martha had guts, unlike me. She didn't tolerate any guff from anyone. I admired her tremendously. She was a highly skilled, experienced emergency room nurse. Energetic, hard-working, and fun, we loved working with her. Highly skilled, intelligent nurses were in big demand, giving them a little leeway. 'Supply and Demand' worked in their favor. On the other hand, if a doctor ever complained of lab, we usually got into trouble. Although not unheard of, our chief lab tech only rarely supported us against a doctor. Martha could have handled the mess with this surgeon, I was sure, unlike me. She wouldn't have been afraid of him.

"You're purposely trying to make me look bad!" the hand surgeon bellowed at me.

That's what he thought? No wonder he was so mad. "No, really, I'm not!"

The fear gripping me must have reflected on my face, convincing him of my sincerity. He softened a little. "Do you think you can do it right from now on?"

"Yes, I'm sure."

Somehow we got through until he finished. On his way out the door, he said to me, "Sorry I was so short earlier. I haven't had dinner yet and I'm hungry."

Well, I'm a forgiving person. No hard feelings. Obviously, he had no plans to get "Martha" into trouble. He was even kinda' sweet right then. So I smiled and said, "No problem. Merry Christmas!"

He stopped, gave me the oddest look, then stormed out the door.

I couldn't get his odd expression out of my mind. What did I do or say again to upset him this time?

And then it hit me. He was Jewish. I hadn't even thought about that.

Ah, well, guess I couldn't do a thing right by him. It just wasn't meant to be.

As I read the written follow-up instructions to the patient's father, he said to me, "I refuse to step foot in that jerk's office. I'll find another doctor to take out my son's stitches. Can you give me the name of a different hand surgeon?"

Good luck! "I understand and empathize with your feelings, sir," I explained, "but unfortunately, doctors are kind of funny about following up another doctor's work. Hand surgeons are a real specialty and this doctor is very good. You're better off to just see him."

The man shook his head and left with his son. I knew he'd never find another specialist to see. Yes, the doctor could be a jerk at times, but he did excellent work. And that's what counted. Nobody paid him to be nice. I had forgiven him. I knew what it was like to work without having eaten. I could get grouchy myself when my blood sugar level dropped.

I was nervous what my friend Martha would think if she discovered I had used her name. I had to tell her. The next time I worked with Martha, I confessed my sin to her.

She just laughed. Whew. I would have hated for my actions to cause any friction between us because I truly liked and respected her. Of course, I would have stepped up and confessed if the incident had caused any trouble for her, which it didn't.

Thank God she had a sense of humor and it didn't affect our friendship. We eventually traveled to California along with two co-workers, stayed in a hotel, and saw Phantom of the Opera. Another time we and two other co-workers visited Las Vegas, gambled, stayed in a hotel, and saw the sights. It was fun to be a part of their team.

***

Occasionally, an outpatient visited our facility. Outpatients are people who do not see our emergency doctor. They come bearing a prescription from their personal doctor for a lab test, an x-ray, or a medication/injection from the nurse.

The receptionist buzzed me. "I registered an outpatient for lab testing."

I brought the young woman back and had her sit on a bed. She was nice-looking and quiet but friendly. She didn't appear to be in any dire distress but looked very uncomfortable. She said her hands were tingling. The requisition from her family doctor next door requested an ABG—Arterial Blood Gas.

Drawing an artery is completely different from drawing a vein. Arteries are surrounded by nerves. If you hit a nerve while drawing the blood sample, there is potential for nerve damage. The patient usually experiences pain when blood gases are drawn. They require a lot of skill to draw. The sample needs to be handled with care because it cannot be exposed to the atmosphere.

I drew blood from her pulsing artery. She winced but held still. I ran the test. Her pH registered high—7.60. Normal arterial blood pH is between 7.38 and 7.42. Her carbon dioxide level read lower than normal. These readings indicated a hyper-ventilator. When a person hyperventilates, he/she exhales too much CO_2. Carbon dioxide is an acid. When the body gets rid of too much of this acid by hyperventilating, the blood's pH becomes too alkaline—in this case, 7.60. A tingling sensation in the hands and feet is a typical symptom.

I called the doctor's office to report the results as requested. The doctor got on the line and I related my findings.

"Okay, that's fine. Tell her she can go home," he said.

Go home? He wasn't going to treat her? I ventured to ask, "Would you like me to tell her to breathe into a paper sack before she leaves?" Breathing into a paper sack allows you to recapture the lost CO_2, thereby normalizing your CO_2 level and subsequently your pH. Then you will lose the tingling sensation in your hands and feet.

He sounded surprised when he answered. "A paper sack? No. She's just hyperventilating. Just send her home. She's fine," he said and hung up.

I didn't understand his response. Didn't he grasp the concept of hyperventilation? I guess I was used to our intelligent ER doctors.

I looked at the miserable girl on the bed, rubbing her tingling hands. I couldn't send her home in that condition. So I found a paper sack and brought it over to her, telling her to breathe into it for a while. I explained to her to focus on slow breathing and stayed beside her until she started to feel better. Finally, the tingling sensation subsided and she left, thanking me.

I made a mental note never to see that family doctor or send anyone else to him. Gaining knowledge of private doctors in the area provided me with one big advantage. I could decide for myself who was good and who to avoid.

With only a couple of exceptions, I liked and respected our emergency room doctors. I wished they had private practices but of course they didn't. One of the smartest ER doctors I ever met in my life was Dr. Pete, a good-looking man in his thirties. The first time

I met him, he told me a story I never forgot.

"A woman had diarrhea for months," he said. "No matter what her doctors tried, nothing worked. They discovered she had no normal flora.

"So finally, they tried something desperate. She had been married for years, so they figured she and her husband shared similar flora. They took her husband's feces and made a suspension of it and flushed it into the woman's colon, thereby providing her with her husband's normal bacteria. The treatment worked. After months of suffering, her diarrhea corrected itself."

I sat listening to his story, thinking, *What an odd story to tell someone you've just met*. But it was interesting. And funny. I think you must possess a strange sense of humor to work in the medical field. And working with this doctor was always interesting.

One night Dr. Pete, and the nurse, the receptionist and I left together at eleven p.m., locking the doors and setting the alarm. Our nurse was an overweight woman in her fifties. The receptionist was a tiny girl, about twenty. X-ray had already left four hours earlier, having remained on stand-by while at home. The four of us walked to our cars in the dark, lonely parking lot and waited to make sure everyone's car started so we could all leave safely. That night, our doctor's sports car wouldn't start.

Even at eleven p.m., warm air surrounded us that summer evening. Batteries frequently give their owners grief in our desert heat.

"We'll push you until it starts," I offered. We all liked this doctor so we were happy to help him. "Just pop the clutch and after we get some speed, it should start."

The nurse, receptionist and I pushed and pushed. He kept popping the clutch, but nothing happened. It proved tough on our nurse because of her weight and she had a sore ankle but she was a good sport. Our tiny receptionist threw her whole body into the job. We stopped to take a breather before we started pushing again. Still nothing. Panting, we rested against the car to catch our breaths before starting again. Sweat dripped down all of our foreheads.

It was strange our efforts weren't working. When I was growing up in the sixties, many of our cars had clutches and many of them had trouble starting. This procedure had always worked.

Then a thought occurred to me. *No, certainly it couldn't be*! But he was young, and we were out of breath and it was getting very late, so I had to ask. "Pete, you do have it in first gear, don't you?"

He looked a little confused. "No, I put it in neutral."

The nurse and I groaned. My head dropped into my hands. No wonder it wasn't starting! "You've gotta put it in first gear!"

"Oh!" He quickly switched gears and we pushed once more. He popped the clutch and in a matter of seconds, the car spat and sputtered, jerking along the empty parking lot, until it finally caught. He zoomed away, waving his thanks.

"You owe us a pizza!" I called out after him.

He was one of the smartest physicians I have ever met in my life, and I would trust my life and the lives of my loved ones to him. But I wouldn't ever trust my car in his hands!

***

I tried to take my short vacations in the summertime. While escaping the Arizona heat, Amy and I went to Minnesota to visit my family and longtime friends. We stayed at my family's lakeside cabin my father built in the 1950s. My siblings and their broods gathered there for swimming, waterskiing, tubing, croquet and pancake breakfasts grilled outdoors.

I have five siblings and Amy connected with her many Minnesota cousins, aunts and uncles. After a day of play and barbecued dinners, we all sat in the screened-in family room to play cards and watch the sun slip behind the sparkling water.

We took a day to drive to Red Wing, MN. I wanted to show Amy the hospital in which she was born. It sat high on a hill, overlooking the mighty Mississippi River. Rolling green hills, various kinds of trees—elms, pines, oaks—and blooming flowers stood everywhere.

"This is it. I remember having a beautiful view out my bedside window," which was nice since I had such a difficult delivery with problems afterwards that I had to stay in the hospital for eight days. Historic buildings and hotels filled the quaint town. We had fun having lunch and exploring antique shops.

I originally left Minnesota to escape bad memories of my pregnancy. I had a hard time forgetting the nightmares I had before she was born—of flying vultures swooping down and grabbing my baby as it was being born. Or my baby being grabbed by some doctors and I never saw it.

But if I remembered back far enough I had many happy memories of my youth. Returning to my childhood summer home reminded me of those good times many years ago and made me feel grounded. Here was where I felt secure. It helped me remember the carefree, happy summers when I was growing up when my only worry was the weather. That's what I focused on.

Where were my heart and home now? Minnesota, where I was raised, where my roots were? Hawaii, the place I also loved and always would? Or Arizona, where I lived now? I didn't know. Then one year I returned from a ten-day vacation in Minnesota and unlocked the door to my Arizona house. As I entered my living room, a warm thought popped into my head. "It's good to be home." This unfamiliar thought surprised me. It had taken years for me to get to that point but I finally felt Arizona was my home, where I planned to stay—a place that made me happy.

Mike had a lot to do with that feeling. As I got to know Mike better, things we had in common came to light. We liked the same music, shared the same taste in movies, enjoyed the same activities. Mike was kind and thoughtful. Over time, we began talking daily and I found myself missing him in-between the times we got together. He was always in my thoughts and heart.

Amy also liked Mike. She was growing more and more independent. One of her hobbies was sewing. A dear family friend of ours taught her how to sew because I had no talent in that area. Amy sewed a pillow for me that said MOM on it, which I treasured. Besides pillows and Christmas ornaments, she sewed a beautiful mint-green taffeta gown and wore it to a convention in New Mexico. My little girl, growing up!

Where had the years gone? Many of them were spent struggling financially, working odd hours, holidays, overtime and for awhile, two jobs. Having a medical career had fascinated me but I wished I could've spent more time at home.

I was glad I had Mike in my life, now that Amy was older and spending more time with friends. I sometimes wished she was still a toddler and I could have all those years again. They had gone by too quickly.

Before I met Mike, I had only traveled to Hawaii, Minnesota and its neighboring states, and Arizona. Mike, a bachelor with no children, had traveled extensively around the world during his life. He came to me one day and asked, "Would you like to go with me to Las Vegas for a few days?" A smile tugged at his mouth and he couldn't hide a glimmer in his eye.

"Sure," I said, but wondered about the look on his face. What was he up to?

Amy stayed with my parents. We drove five hours to Vegas, crossing Hoover Dam on our way, and would stay in a deluxe suite in Caesar's Palace. The drive itself was lovely. The city of Las Vegas glittered with excitement.

I loved our suite. Spacious rooms. King-sized soft bed. Mammoth bathtub with whirlpool jets. Nice view of the strip.

As I reveled in the luxury of our room, he suddenly turned to face me. A hopeful look came into his eyes and he grinned. He acted like he knew something that I didn't know.

"What's going on?" I asked him.

"Will you marry me?"

What a sweetie! I wasn't too surprised however because I knew we'd get married sometime. We loved each other. The only question in my mind had been when it would happen. It's about time, I thought. We were soul mates in many ways. I threw my arms around him. "Yes." No other man made me as happy.

Hoping I would say "Yes," he had already made arrangements with the Candlelight Wedding Chapel and also obtained tickets for two shows, *Cirque du Soleil* and *Siegfried and Roy*. He had everything planned.

We went to the courthouse to get a license. The weather was perfect that October day. We walked around, holding hands in a romantic, young-love state of mind, trying to find the courthouse but were lost. We saw a small bus parked in a drive-way tucked away from the street. An official-looking woman sat behind the wheel.

I'd never known Mike to ever ask anyone for directions, anywhere. He surprised me when he walked up to the bus with me following behind him and knocked on the bus door. It swished open. "Can you tell me where the courthouse is?" Mike asked the driver. I stood next to him, waiting.

Male whistles and cat-calls came from the back of the bus.

What the heck?

"Shaddup!" The female driver yelled to the men in back. A tough cookie.

Oh, no! Of all the people to ask for directions, we had stumbled upon a bus full of criminals. There they sat in striped clothes and handcuffs, whistling and yelling at us. "Woo, woo. Getting married, are we?"

"Got yourself a hot one, buddy!"

"Bet you can't wait!"

The driver yelled, "I said shaddup!" She then turned to us and said in a sweet voice, "It's right around the corner."

"Oh, thanks." We walked away as quickly as we could, our faces hot with embarrassment, whistles following us. The bus door whooshed shut and we rounded the corner, leaving the prisoners behind us.

The Hispanic female Methodist minister at the chapel radiated spirituality. Both of us liked her. She blessed us and our union. Some people wrinkle their noses when I tell them we got married in Vegas, but the ceremony proved lovelier than what I imagined could be possible there. The chapel supplied everything—music, flowers, even a blue garter. That night we ate dinner in an Italian restaurant, Trevi, at Caesar's Palace and sat next to a beautiful fountain. Later that week we enjoyed the two magnificent shows. All in all, we had a fabulous time.

Our marriage didn't surprise my family. They all liked Mike. Amy was very happy for us.

In late December, we took Amy on a trip to Washington D.C., visited the Smithsonian Museum and met one of Mike's brothers in New Jersey. The three of us also visited Williamsburg and spent New Year's Eve on Chesapeake Bay watching the boats light up with Christmas lights, twinkling on the water in the darkness of the night. Fireworks and firecrackers hailed the New Year.

I tingled all over at the beautiful sight and looked forward to a lifetime with Mike.

***

A few days of annual vacation always zipped by too quickly. It was a good thing I enjoyed my job. That was the key to putting up with crazy hours and the stress. Our regular doctors were easy to talk to, since we got to know them fairly well working side by side with them. Occasionally, a doctor from the hospital that owned us came to our emergency center to fill in a shift. We didn't know those doctors very well.

One of the fill-in docs was a physician who acted very aloof. He stayed in the doctor's room until we buzzed him to come out to see a patient. When finished, he went straight back to the doctor's room and closed the door. He didn't smile or even talk to us. I noticed he was quite chatty on the phone, however, when talking to another doctor. I was glad he didn't work at our center very often.

On a different day, his ex-wife worked with us. She was a nurse from Phoenix Desert Hospital filling in for one of our regular nurses on vacation. We sat talking in the lounge. Somehow, the conversation got around to this fill-in-nurse's ex-husband the aloof doctor. After the x-ray tech and I told her about our difficulty in talking to her ex-husband, she said, "He did have his good points in our marriage, however. I never had an orgasm before in my life before I married him."

The female x-ray tech and I froze, too stunned to react. We then agreed our negative impression of that doctor suddenly changed to one very positive. That particular attribute rated pretty high in our opinion.

We now had a new-found respect for this aloof doctor.

We loved most of our regular doctors. They took care of us and we took care of them. Sometimes we brought homemade dishes for lunch when our favorite doctors were on duty.

One afternoon, three of us—our nurse, x-ray tech, and I—sat lined up on the couch in our staff lounge. Three women, all in our thirties or forties, taking a break between patients. We each had a book to read and were trying to snatch a few pages before the next inevitable onslaught of patients swooped in.

One of our good-looking ER doctors who was in his early

thirties and his wife entered the front door. He wanted to be examined by our ER doc on duty that day. Evidently the patient/doctor had a rectal problem. The two doctors went into the gynecology room for the exam, the only room at the center with a door they could close for privacy, as opposed to just a curtain.

The three of us on the couch didn't think anything of this at all. We'd seen everything in the ER. Think of something wild—we've seen it. Now think of something one hundred times worse—we've seen it. Things I'd never write about. We just hoped the doctor's little butt was okay. Who among us hasn't had a butt problem upon occasion? No big deal. We just hoped everything was all right.

We didn't pay much attention or give any thought to the exam going on in the gyn room. We're professionals after all. We focused on our books. The quiet in the room was only occasionally broken by the rustling sound of pages turning during our break.

We three ladies sat quietly minding our own business, when after a while the patient/doctor's wife walked into the lounge. Good -looking, she exuded an untamed sexiness.

"Hi," we all said in turn.

Always friendly to us, the doctor's wife smiled her hello and nodded, then walked over to the sink and placed a glass in it for us to wash for her.

The wife started to leave the room when suddenly she whirled around and exclaimed, "I never shoved anything weird up there."

The three of us looked up, startled at the sudden outburst. I'm sure all our jaws dropped and our eyes popped open wide as we sat staring at the defensive look crossing the wife's face. We didn't know what to say, so we said nothing.

Then, just as suddenly, she whirled back around and left.

Methinks the lady doth protest too much.

That thought had never occurred to any of us. Until she mentioned it.

Then we couldn't get the thought out of our minds.

I guess he was all right because he eventually exited the room and left. We three on the couch looked at each other and shrugged. We vowed we had seen nothing. Heard nothing. Would say nothing.

Which was pretty good for us blabbermouths.

**

An elderly gentleman patient came in one day. After our receptionist generated a chart, our female x-ray tech took his vital signs and medical history. Everyone loved to work with her—very pretty, skilled, good sense of humor, intelligent and hard-working. The male doctors especially loved working with her. I think they liked looking at her. And she told the best jokes.

She walked to the nurse's station and handed the patient's chart to our doctor, one of our favorites. Our doctor that day was a balding, elderly man with years of experience. We loved to work with him because he was smart, efficient and pleasant. None of us could figure out why he had five ex-wives.

"What's his complaint?" the doctor asked.

"He has gas," the x-ray tech said. Before she could get out another word, the doctor exited the station and walked over to the patient, without even looking at the chart. He trusted our x-ray tech.

"Omigosh!" she said.

"What?" I asked.

"I was just joking when I said he has gas. He just has an earache." She buried her face in her hands. "I can't look."

I sat in the nurse's station on a stool and watched the scene through the glass window.

"I understand you've got some gas?" our doctor asked the patient at the bedside.

The man looked shocked. We all waited for the doctor to blow his top at being misled. Or the patient to be offended.

Then the man's eyes opened wide and he replied, "Why, yes, I do!"

"Well, we'll take care of that for you." The doctor started to walk away when the man said, "I have an earache, too."

"Let me see." The doctor grabbed an otoscope and looked into the man's ear. "Yes, it's infected all right. We'll get you all fixed up."

Our nurse gave the man some Mylanta for his gas. The doctor

wrote a prescription for the earache. Our x-ray tech gave him his follow-up instructions. I cleaned the bedside area. The man left happy. One of the most satisfied customers we've ever had.

We never told the doctor the patient hadn't mentioned his gas. The patient must have thought our doctor was the smartest man he ever met, with insight unknown to other mere mortal men.

***

Occasionally I worked with a male x-ray tech who filled in for vacations at our emergency center. He told me one of the worst things I've ever heard. It happened one night before I began working there. He said a young couple rushed into our center with a three-year-old limp girl in their arms. Frantic, they shouted, "She fell out the back door of our car as we were driving home from camping. We couldn't stop fast enough. We ran over her. Oh, God, please save her!"

Our emergency center crew wasted no time. They placed the child on the bed. She wasn't breathing, her skin was blue. Our ER doctor opened her mouth to intubate but saw a mass of gray matter in the child's throat. He couldn't even begin to try to save her. Her brains were mush.

Her parents stood a few feet away, hoping beyond hope their child would be saved. The mother bit her nails and wailed. The father looked sick. They clung to each other and watched with horrified looks on their faces. It was the early 1980s, before the big push for car seats and seat belts, so we couldn't judge these people.

Our x-ray tech, himself a father, felt compassion for the mother. He told me she had long dark hair, falling past her shoulders. Small specks of gray matter scattered throughout her hair.

He knew immediately what it was. He didn't want her to go home and look in the mirror and have it slowly dawn on her that her daughter's brains were strewn throughout her hair. So he tried to pick the specks out of the mother's long hair without her growing suspicious about his actions. He continued this surreptitious task until he couldn't see any more gray matter in her hair. Fortunately, she was too distraught to notice what he was doing.

The doctor pronounced the child DOA. Every time I think of that incident, I shiver. If that ever happened to my daughter, I'd freak and go into a deep depression. Those poor parents. Thankfully the public has been educated to the importance of car seats and seat belts since then. But that poor couple had to return home without their beloved little daughter. I wasn't even there that night but my heart ached for them.

***

A twenty-five-year old male knelt in our lobby, doubled over, clutching his ribs. "Help me! Help me! Oh, the pain. I can't stand the pain!" Anguish covered his face. Because of his loud screams piercing the air, I immediately brought him back to a bed, before the other patients who sat in the lobby quietly waiting their turn to be brought back for their medical problems.

The patient stumbled to the bed and crawled on top, lying on his side in a fetal position. "Oh, God, help me. Please help me."

I tried to get information out of him but it was sketchy. "Just give me something for the pain!"

His blood pressure read normal. His heart rate registered normal. His skin felt cool and dry. *Hmmm, that's odd for someone in so much pain.*

Our doctor examined him, then ordered an x-ray. The patient limped down the hallway to the x-ray department, doubled over, moaning the entire way.

After the x-ray tech took the picture, the patient returned to his bed and resumed his moaning.

The x-ray revealed no abnormality.

I brought the man his written follow-up instructions from our doctor. "Rest. Tylenol for the pain. See your family doctor as needed."

The guy jumped off the bed, furious and started screaming. "Tylenol? I need something more for the pain!" He stood straight up, waving his arms. "This place sucks s***, man. You guys are a bunch of f***ing quacks!" He shouted at the top of his lungs. He threw the instruction sheet on the floor and marched out with his girlfriend.

I watched him leave and thought, Look at that! His pain

seems to have suddenly disappeared. He's walking just fine now.

We were truly miracle workers.

A different afternoon, a pretty blonde woman in her thirties came in complaining of pain. She wore a colorful sundress with a flower print and pink jelly sandals.

She hopped up on the bed and smiled at our doctor on duty that day. "Dr. B" we called him. Everybody loved Dr. B. Overweight, white hair, friendly southern drawl, he looked like Santa Claus. Not only was he a good, caring doctor, but he was also generous, always buying dinner for the staff.

The woman swayed a little as she sat on the bed and crossed her legs. Her words slurred as she spoke. She knew Dr. B personally because her husband worked for the hospital. She placed her hand on Dr. B's chest and patted him. "Hi there!," she said, in an attempt to flirt with him. "I really need something for my pain. Be an angel, won't you, and write me a prescription?"

Dr. B looked at her and uttered one word. "No."

Her pretty little face screwed itself into a scowl and her lips formed a pout. She pushed him away. "You old poop!"

Dr. B just shook his head and walked away. Evidently this wasn't the first time she had tried this with him and other doctors. No one could ever find the source of her 'pain'.

We loved Dr. B! A very caring and experienced doctor, a drug-seeker couldn't fool him. He was one smart man.

I wished Dr. B had been on duty the day a drunk male in his twenties came in with his buddy. "I think I broke my foot," the drunk said. He hobbled to the bed and lay down, moaning in pain.

I did the usual treatment—propped his foot up on a pillow and applied a bag of ice. A tiny amount of swelling and discoloration showed on the top part of his foot. "How did you injure your foot?" I asked.

"Kicked my dog."

My face must have registered my surprise and distaste because he burst out laughing. "Looks like we got ourselves a dog lover here," he said to his buddy. His buddy didn't respond and looked embarrassed.

I wanted to scream in anger at the patient but needed to maintain a professional demeanor. Frustrated, I wrote on the chart,

"Patient states pain in left foot, from kicking his dog," and handed the chart to our doctor on duty that day.

Our x-ray tech that particular shift was busy with another patient so we had to wait for the film. In the meantime, our doctor ordered a shot of Demerol to ease the patient's pain.

As far as I was concerned, if the guy hurt his foot kicking his dog, let him suffer. He deserved the pain. Not very compassionate of me but I couldn't conjure up any sympathy for the guy. Yes, I was a dog lover.

The nurse told me, "All I can do is stall as long as I can, but I have to eventually give him his pain shot." She felt the same way I did about the patient.

After the x-ray tech finished with him, the doctor diagnosed "Hematoma." A fancy word for nothing but a bruise. The guy got a shot of Demerol for a bruise he received from kicking his dog.

I wanted to report the patient to ASPCA but I couldn't because that would've been a violation of patient confidentiality.

Sickening. I didn't like that particular doctor to begin with and after that incident I liked him even less.

The patient left in a state of contented bliss.

***

Because of the frequent flow of drug-seeking patients through emergency rooms, it could be difficult at times for doctors to weed out the drug-seekers from the real patients.

One afternoon, the receptionist handed me a chart listing the patient's complaint. "Pain all over." He was an African-American male in his twenties, with a polite, quiet manner, even though he was doubled over in pain.

He hobbled back to an exam room and could barely crawl onto the bed. I took his vital signs, recording them on the chart. Both his blood pressure and pulse read high. I asked all the necessary questions. "Allergies to any medications? Taking any medications? History of any illnesses?"

"Sickle cell disease," he said. "I need some pain medication."

Wow. If he was in a crisis right then, that would explain his pain.

Our ER doctor that day went in to examine him, then came

out and wrote CBC—Complete Blood Count—on the chart in the space saved for lab orders.

I drew the patient's blood and took the sample back to my lab to analyze. I immediately made a smear. While the slide dried, I diluted the blood and ran the sample through the Coulter. The machine sucked and aspirated as the blood gurgled its way through various tubing and apertures for readings.

His hemoglobin read low indicating anemia. The red blood cell indices registered abnormal readings consistent with sickle cell anemia. I repeated the test and got the same results, then performed the necessary steps to stain the slide and examined it under the microscope. Sure enough, sickled red cells dotted numerous fields. No surprise there. He definitely was in a crisis.

Sickle cell anemia is an inherited disease, where the gene causes the body to make abnormal hemoglobin in the red cells. Sickled red cells are shaped like a sickle, instead of the normal round doughnut shape. This causes them to occasionally form clumps in the bloodstream, blocking blood flow through the patient's blood vessels and organs, causing pain.

Our doctor walked into the lab as I wrote my report. "So, what do you have?"

I showed him my report. "He's in a crisis, all right." It was exciting to help diagnose such an unusual disease. Many of our patients at the emergency facility had minor problems, with only an occasional interesting case. It made me feel good to be able to identify a sickle cell crisis and be part of the medical team to help this man.

But our young doctor looked disturbed, almost irritated. His weight shifted from one foot to the other. "Let me look at the smear, okay?"

"Sure." Always happy to help a doctor learn what I was looking at, I positioned the slide back under the microscope for him.

He peered into the lens, examining various parts of the slide. I expected him to say, "Oh, I see," but instead, he said, "Do you know what oat cells are?"

Oat cells? Of course I know what oat cells are. They're called that because some red blood cells are shaped like a grain of oat instead of a doughnut. But any certified hematology lab tech would be able to differentiate an oat cell from a sickled cell. There was no way those were oat cells.

"Yes." I smiled politely as I answered his inane question. This particular doctor and I got along quite well and I considered him a friend so I treaded carefully.

"You don't think these are just oat cells?" he persisted. I could tell he wanted to believe that. Dear Lord, how on earth could he say that? How could I let him know that was an idiotic question without sounding rude? "No, they're definitely sickled," I said.

My answer didn't make him happy. I knew he thought this patient was just another drug seeker, faking pain to get drugs. Because many drug addicts came in to emergency rooms seeking drugs, our doctors sometimes became cynical about patients in pain. Some of these patients can be quite good actors. But this young man was not faking anything. I was sure of it.

Because of my findings, our doctor was obligated to send the patient to Phoenix Desert Hospital for further testing and treatment. The doctor seemed glad to transfer the patient into someone else's hands. I sent a tube of blood over to the main lab for hemoglobin electrophoresis to test for abnormal hemoglobin, and also sent the smear for the pathologist to review.

But our ER doctor didn't give the patient anything for his pain. I knew he still thought the patient was faking the pain and didn't believe my report. I had always had a good relationship with this doctor, and still do to this day, but it irritated me that he didn't believe my professional findings. I was the expert in this case, not him. Maybe he just didn't want to. Many doctors get angry at drug seekers who try to use them to feed their habit.

We didn't hear anything more about our young man that night because it was getting late and we closed at eleven p.m. That's one of the things about working in an emergency center I didn't like. You usually don't get to find out what happens to a patient. You see them in a crisis situation and then they're transferred and you don't have anything to do with them anymore. But sometimes there are ways of finding out.

The next day I received a note in the inter-office mail from my pathologist, the doctor of the main hospital's laboratory. He confirmed my findings, stating that I had done an excellent job reading the smear.

The hemoglobin electrophoresis showed Hemoglobin S, the hemoglobin causing Sickle Cell Anemia. I called Admitting at the hospital and discovered our young man was admitted and treated at the hospital for his crisis.

I kept the note from my pathologist. I wanted to keep it and put it in my file. It wasn't often that one gets a note from a pathologist commending one's work. It made me feel good.

***

A co-worker told me the following story. On a quiet Monday evening when I was off, our center's one patient was being x-rayed for a sore arm. No one waited in the waiting room. The automatic front door slid open and a nice-looking male in his twenties walked in. There was nothing unusual about him. He went up to our sixty-year-old sweet receptionist just inside the front door and calmly said in a low, quiet voice, "I have a gun. I want narcotics."

Our receptionist had a clear head. She stared at him for a second in disbelief then nodded and led him to the back. The doctor and nurse sat in the nurse's station behind a glass window waiting for the x-ray tech to finish with their one patient. The male x-ray tech and patient were in the x-ray department located around the corner, at the end of a hallway from the nurse's station. The lab tech talked on the phone in the lounge around the other corner from the nurse's station.

"This gentleman has a gun. He wants narcotics," our receptionist said to the doctor. The man opened his jacket, revealing a gun tucked into the waist of his jeans.

Stunned, it took a moment for them to react. The doctor then nodded to the nurse. She took out her key and went into the brightly lit medication room, which wasn't any bigger than a small closet, adjacent to the nurse's station.

"Stay here," the gunman ordered our receptionist. He stood in the doorway to the med room facing our nurse and watched while she unlocked the drawers. He didn't say a word, just stood there quietly and waited.

The phone rang. "Don't answer that," the gunman ordered. It

145

rang and rang, cutting sharply through the silence and then suddenly stopped.

Our doctor sat motionless and stared out the large glass window surrounding the nurse's station. Soon, our sharp x-ray tech emerged from the x-ray department and made his way down the hallway toward the nurse's station with an x-ray in his hand. Fortunately, he glanced at the glass window as he walked. Without moving his head, our doctor mouthed the words, "CALL THE POLICE" and opened his eyes wide.

That's all it took for our smart x-ray tech to instantly assess the situation. As I think of this, I always admire that guy's quick-witted action. He quietly turned around and tip-toed back down the hallway and through the door to his department, without being seen or heard by the gunman.

The nurse stalled. The gunman watched her. The x-ray tech kept the patient in the x-ray department. The lab tech was fortunately safe in the lounge, unaware of the events. The doctor and receptionist sat motionless in the nurse's station.

It didn't take long for the police to arrive. Our brave nurse was just finishing emptying the drawers of narcotics when the cops yelled, "POLICE! Put your hands up!" The gunman slowly put his hands in the air. They cuffed him and led him away.

There had been a rash of burglarized emergency rooms in the previous few months throughout the valley. Thanks to our brave little staff, and especially our alert x-ray tech, the culprit had been captured.

I never thought about the possibility of danger while working in these emergency centers. When I heard this story, all I could think was, *Wow, I'm glad I wasn't there the night this incident happened.* Thank God the lab tech didn't come out of the lounge, for her sake. I always felt safe but now I realized that, although rare, something could potentially happen. We had no security guard. Our main hospital miles away crawled with police officers of course, but not us, we were too small to warrant security. Once in a while, a patrolling police officer stopped in for a cup of coffee. I didn't think about danger. I tended toward optimism and didn't allow negative situations to rule my life. Guess we got lucky because that was the only time a gunman threatened any of our three free-standing emergency centers in the nearly thirteen years I worked at them.

***

Because not all emergency room patients require lab work, I only performed lab tests part of my work-day. Therefore, the hospital had cross-trained me to do a variety of things to help the nurse and x-ray tech. I loaded x-ray films, applied splints to broken legs and arms, bandaged wounds, flushed out eyes with bags of saline, opened sterile trays, soaked paranychia—infected nail beds—in hydrogen peroxide, did EKG's, applied oxygen, gave tetanus shots, mini-catheterized patients for urine samples, performed CPR on heart attack victims, and held eyes open while the doctor drilled, yes, drilled, rust out of the pupils. Every time I assisted with that particular procedure, the room spun around and I had to force myself not to faint. Never got used to it.

I also did outpatient lab tests. In and out. These patients didn't see the ER doctor. They simply came in for a lab test.

I brought back an outpatient lab patient one day to draw his blood. He was an ordinary looking, middle-aged businessman. Dark hair, glasses, neatly dressed. With a flat abdomen and muscular arms, he looked like he worked out. His doctor had ordered a CBC. I was a one-man-lab-phlebotomist and technologist rolled into one.

"Just hop up onto the bed, sir. Would you like to lie down?" I asked.

"No thanks, I'll sit up. That's fine." He rolled up his sleeve and sat up on the bed.

I palpated for a vein, readied my supplies, applied the tourniquet, and inserted the needle. As his blood squirted into the vacutainer, he suddenly began to jerk. His eyes rolled back into his head and he slumped forward.

"Help!" I called out, hoping either our nurse or x-ray tech would hear me. I struggled with the man as he started to slip off the bed. The needle was still in his vein. If I took it out right then, his blood would squirt all over because the tourniquet still compressed his arm. But I couldn't release the tourniquet because I needed my free hand to hold onto him so he didn't fall off the bed.

Suddenly, his glasses fell off and flew directly down, landing in the portable small waste can below with a clunk. Bull's eye. His body convulsed more violently.

"Help! Bed Seven!" I cried out more loudly. Everything seemed to happen in slow motion before speeding up.

Then our wonderful nurse and x-ray tech both rushed into the room. Now I could rip the tourniquet off his arm and maneuver the needle out, without poking myself or anyone else and without making too much of a mess. The nurse and x-ray tech pulled him back onto the bed and laid him down with his feet propped up. Teamwork.

Soon, color returned to my patient's face and he blinked his eyes. "What happened?"

"You fainted while I was drawing your blood."

He shook his head in vehement denial. "No. I didn't. I would never faint."

I retrieved his glasses from the metal waste can and handed them to him. "Here are your glasses. They fell off when you fainted."

He put them on and gave me an indignant look. "I didn't faint."

I decided to drop the matter. "Fortunately, I got enough blood to run the test so I don't need to stick you again. You lie here for a while and rest. When you're feeling better, you can leave."

"I'm fine right now." Stubborn man! He got up and I walked him out, not wanting him to pass out again. He couldn't get out of there fast enough.

When I was a student, the school assigned me to work in a medical clinic to practice drawing blood. One of my male patients, probably in his forties, sat in the drawing chair. I flipped the chair's arm over in front of him, locking him in place then drew his blood. As soon as he saw his blood shoot into the vacutainer tube, he started to convulse. Fortunately, he was in a chair behind a locked-in arm so I could manage him and get the tourniquet off and needle out of his vein.

When he came to, I asked him if he was all right. "Of course I am, why wouldn't I be?" He blinked and sat up straight, looking around.

"You passed out when I drew your blood."

A shocked look crossed his face then switched to an angry expression. "No I didn't," he vehemently denied.

Sure. I made it up.

Sometimes I just don't understand some men. One of our ER doctors, one I didn't like which was rare, used to bring in dirty movies for us—the nurse, x-ray and lab—to watch in-between patients. Yuk. I wasn't interested and always found cleaning and/or stocking to do while the movie ran so I didn't have to watch it. Unless a male nurse happened to work that shift, the doctor was the only one watching. One night we were all talking with that particular doctor in the lounge and he made a comment about women being the weaker sex.

"Well," I piped in, "in all my years of drawing blood, I've had only three patients faint. And they were all male."

The doctor, middle-aged and overweight, immediately stood up, visibly agitated, shifting his weight from one foot to the other. He gave me a dirty look. "That's not true at all. It's women who faint."

The nurse joined in. "In my entire career, the only patients who've fainted when they saw my needle have been men."

In a huff, the doctor turned and left the lounge, retreating to the doctor's room. Clearly, he didn't wish to hear any more of our tall tales.

Years later, a story circulated throughout the medical profession. At one of the hospitals in the valley, a fire fighter needed a shot in his hip. The nurse asked him to lie down on the bed but he refused. He insisted on standing, leaning against the bed instead. As soon as he saw the needle, he passed out and collapsed on the floor. He fell in such a way that he fractured his neck, paralyzing himself. He sued that hospital.

Lesson to all medical personnel: Be in charge of your patient. Don't let them tell you what they want. You tell them what to do.

The cutest four-year-old girl came in one day, needing stitches. She lay perfectly still as the doctor injected lidocaine into the area to numb it and then sewed her up. She cooperated fully every step of the way. As I was giving her mother the follow-up instructions, a man and his young son came in to the next bed. From the other side of the curtain, we could hear the little boy wailing and making a fuss.

The father said, "Now, son. You have to be brave. Don't be like a girl and cry. Only girls cry. Be a big boy while the doctors and nurses take care of you." But the boy kept crying.

As my brave little female patient and her mother readied to leave, I told the young girl, speaking in a voice loud enough to make sure I could be heard on the other side of the curtain, "You were such a brave girl! The bravest patient we've ever had. Braver than any other boy or girl I've ever seen."

I walked with them as they left, past the bed with the father and crying son. I glanced their way. The father turned his head and saw me. A sheepish expression appeared on his face.

Might as well set that little boy straight early in his life about little girls, I thought.

Years later, my four-year-old grandson was in the hospital for a month with a ruptured appendix and two surgeries. He turned out to be the bravest little patient I have ever known.

***

I enjoyed performing lab tests and I also enjoyed working with patients. One summer evening an elderly woman came in with an injured arm, accompanied by her blind husband. X-rays revealed a fracture.

While the rest of the staff was busy, I splinted the woman's broken arm and eased it into a sling then gave her the discharge instructions. Our nurse asked me to accompany the couple out to their car. I took the patient's good arm and helped her outside. Her blind husband slowly followed, tapping his white cane.

As the three of us shuffled across the dark parking lot, I asked the woman, "Will you be able to drive all right with your broken arm?" I wondered how they arrived in the first place, considering the pain she must have had with her broken arm.

"Oh, I don't know how to drive."

Startled, I stopped and looked at her. Had I misheard her? "But, how will you get home?" Since her husband was blind, the situation completely baffled me. How had they gotten to our emergency center? Had a friend driven them? Did I need to call somebody? All kinds of questions flitted through my mind.

"Oh, my husband will drive. We do this all the time. I just tell him when to turn."

Huh? I reluctantly watched as she helped him into the driver's seat, put his cane into the back seat, then made her way around to the passenger's side and climbed in. She guided his hand to the ignition, he started the engine then off they went. The car jerked and swerved away, toward the busy Friday night main street Phoenix traffic.

Barely believing what I saw, I shook my head. Now that was teamwork at its best.

***

We had to be ready in the emergency center at all times because some of our patients burst through the door with no warning. A couple in their twenties ran in one night yelling, "Help! Our grandma had a heart attack!"

The nurse and I quickly rolled a gurney out to the car, where the elderly lady lay stretched out on the back seat. The couple pulled their grandmother out of the car and onto the gurney. We rushed her into the code room.

Meanwhile our receptionist alerted our doctor and he stood waiting in the code room. He lifted the patient's arm. Stiff.

"She started complaining of chest pain soon after we left Flagstaff. We didn't know of any emergency rooms along the way, so we drove her down here," the young girl said, clinging to the arm of her companion.

From Flagstaff? That's a two hour drive north of us, through the mountains! In the 1980s, our facility was the farthest north in the Phoenix Valley. No other cities of any large size existed between Phoenix and Flagstaff and no other hospitals that I knew of right on the freeway.

Grandma had been dead in the back seat for quite some time. Rigor mortis had already set in. We couldn't do anything for her. Poor Grandma was gone.

I looked at the lady lying on the gurney. She looked peaceful. At least she died surrounded by loved ones.

It made me think of my grandma who died when I was seventeen. She was a loving woman and a great cook. I missed her and took a moment to shoot a little prayer toward heaven for my grandma.

Many sad and tragic things happened while I worked at the emergency centers. I had to build up a wall, like a defense, against getting too emotionally involved with patients. The only way I could maintain my sanity sometimes was to develop an emotional distance. Like the night an entire bridal party rushed in to the center. The bride's long white satin dress swooshed as she moved. Her train flowed easily behind her but her veil couldn't hide the frantic look on her face as her mother was rushed into our code room.

Three girls in matching lilac dresses wandered the hallway just outside our code room, not knowing what to do. Four males in tuxedoes stood helplessly by. One of them put his arm around the bride, consoling her. She stood outside the door to the code room looking in, wringing her hands.

I took in the surreal scene in a second. Most people who came into the emergency centers were not dressed up, much less in a wedding party. What should have been a day of celebration for these people had turned tragic. The mother of the bride had suffered a heart attack.

We instantly went to work, each with our prescribed duties. The doctor intubated the patient and gave oxygen. The nurse started an IV and administered medications. The x-ray tech and I took turns performing CPR. The doctor shocked with paddles but nothing worked. The doctor finally called the code, pronouncing her dead. We looked at the clock on the wall to note the time of death.

The doctor removed the intubation tube. The woman lay on the table in her pretty dress she had probably bought special for her daughter's wedding. Her short brown hair was still in neat curls framing her face. Shoes the same color as her dress remained on her feet. I imagined her getting all dressed up, excited for her daughter's wedding. It made me sick. I wanted to reach out and pat her hand but I didn't.

With looks of disbelief on their faces, the bride and her groom entered the room slowly to say their good-byes. The rest of the party followed with tears flowing down their cheeks, gathered around the gurney, and comforted the bride.

We all felt horrible about this nightmare. It was like walking around in a fog after that until the end of our shift and we could go home and shake it off.

***

If all our patients ended in tragedy, I don't think I could have stayed working there. My nerves wouldn't have stood it but fortunately we were part of a larger team that helped many people and saved lives. A father carried in his young daughter, about ten years old, saying her neck hurt. She was also listless. The father gently placed her on the bed.

Our doctor ordered a CBC. I drew the child's blood and then ran the test. The white count was high, in the twenty thousands. Normal is five to ten thousand. When I looked under the microscope, neutrophils and bands—immature white cells—filled the view. This indicated stress of some kind consumed her body, forcing it to release white cells into her bloodstream so fast they didn't have time to mature in the bone marrow first.

With her symptoms and blood test results, our doctor diagnosed meningitis. We transferred her to the main hospital, Phoenix Desert. Our nurse called the next day and learned the young girl had improved. What a relief. She was on her way to recovery. As a mother myself, I could easily relate to the fear her parents must have felt.

Cute children were my favorite patients. One day a little three -year-old girl came in with her mother who told the receptionist, "I think she stuck a small magnet into her vagina."

I brought the mother and child into the gyn-room. The patient was so quiet and sweet, with blonde curls and blue eyes. Her mother stood next to her, whispering in her ear to keep her calm. The doctor had to perform an exam on her. I set up the exam tray and assisted.

The doctor felt leery about doing an internal exam on a patient this young but he had to. The little girl lay quietly and didn't make a fuss. He could feel the magnet inside her but couldn't get it out. Beads of perspiration collected on the doctor's forehead as he

153

tried to get the blasted thing out of this precious child.

Exasperated, the doctor wiped the sweat off his face. The patient didn't cry or move, just stared at the ceiling and continued to hold very still. I stood helplessly by.

The doctor turned to me and asked, "You wouldn't happen to have a large magnet in the lab, would you? Maybe that will pull it down where I can get a hold of it." I think he was grasping for any kind of help. I didn't have one but felt like running out to the nearest science supply store and buying one with my own money.

Soon the toddler shook her head slightly and said in her soft child's voice, "I'll never stick anything up there again!"

We laughed and agreed that was a good idea. Our doctor gave up. He didn't dare probe too much in case of causing injury. We arranged for a gynecology specialist to meet them at Phoenix Desert's emergency room and take over the exam. Our doctor called over later and learned the gyn-doctor eventually met with success, much to everyone's relief.

***

Mike loved to travel. I'd never been out of the USA but he'd traveled all over the world including Europe, Asia, South America, nearly everywhere with the exception of Hawaii. The two of us flew together to Honolulu for a week. Amy was in school so she remained with my parents. Mike and I stayed in the New Otani Kaimana Hotel on Waikiki Beach. Our room boasted an ocean view. Robert Louis Stevenson had sat under a tree next to that hotel and wrote. I imagined seeing him sitting next to me as I sunbathed, working away on one of his classics.

Because we lived in a dry desert, I wasn't used to the humidity of Hawaii anymore. After showering in our hotel room, I used some powder and accidentally sprinkled some onto the bathroom tile. Mike pointed to my footprint in the powder on the floor. He smiled and sighed. "So cute. Your little footprint."

He admired my footprint? I stared at him. I realized I had the best husband in the world. He was truly wonderful and I was lucky.

We ate dinner one night at their outdoor beachfront restaurant and watched the sun set over the ocean while sailboats drifted in the distance.

We also ate dinner one night at the Oceanarium Restaurant in the Pacific Beach Hotel in Waikiki. Sitting next to a gigantic, two-story floor-to-ceiling aquarium, we watched the divers feed the sting-rays and large fish—one of my favorite places.

Another evening we met Liz and her boyfriend for drinks and a lounge jazz show. It was great seeing Liz again. We talked and got caught up on each other's lives. She worked evenings in a lab dedicated to a hospital's Emergency Room, so our paths had taken similar routes. She and her boyfriend had purchased a condo together. I realized then that both Liz and I had found the loves of our lives and were also both settled into our medical careers. We had much to discuss.

Soon our week in Paradise ended. The flight was supposed to leave Sunday morning. I was scheduled to work a twelve-hour shift Monday. Mike had Monday off. He worked for the state of Arizona in the transportation department as an inspector on road and bridge construction crews.

I called the airlines to check if the flight was leaving on time and discovered the flight was moved to Monday, when I was supposed to work!

I felt helpless, trying to solve this problem all the way over in Hawaii. I didn't know the phone number of our fill-in lab tech. Administration didn't work on Sundays. The only number I knew was the number of the emergency center. Panicking, I called the lab tech who worked opposite days from me. She and I did things for each other, always making sure the lab was clean and stocked for the other person.

"I'm stuck in Hawaii an extra day," I said. "Can you trade days with me? You work Monday for me and I'll work either Tuesday or Wednesday for you?" The two of us alternated twelve-hour days at that time.

"No," she said. "I don't want to trade. But I'll work Monday for you." The hospital would have to pay overtime to her and would force me to use twelve additional hours of my quickly dwindling vacation time.

Can't have everything. Although I would have done it for her. I flew back to Arizona Monday night. She worked her regular Tuesday/Wednesday shifts. Thursday I returned to work. Life in Paradise screeched to a halt. Fortunately, I enjoyed my job and found it stimulating. When I saw my co-workers—the doctor, the nurse, the X-ray tech, the receptionist—it hit me that not only had I missed my daughter but I had also missed my co-workers. I felt lucky to have a fulfilling career with nice people.

***

"Plaster splint needed in Bed One," the nurse said.

I had learned how to make and apply plaster splints. First, I wrapped the limb with a cloth wrap to protect it from the heat of the exothermic reaction of the setting plaster. After that I pulled layers and layers of dry, wide plaster off the supply cart. Bits of dry plaster scattered into the air and little particles of plaster flew into my face. Then I donned gloves and soaked the plaster in a large bucket of water and molded it over a protective wrap on the injured limb. Finally I wrapped an elastic bandage around the hot plaster to hold it in place.

The day after the plaster particles flew into my face, I awoke and my eye throbbed. The plaster had irritated it, setting up an infection. I looked in the mirror. The entire area around my eye was swollen. I had to go to work at eleven a.m.

The doctor on duty that morning remarked, "You look tired." I guess the swelling did make me look tired. The pain continued all day.

At seven p.m., the day-shift doctor left. Dr. B, our doctor who looked like Santa Claus, came on duty for the next twelve-hour shift. He took one look at me and said, "You've got cellulitis." He wrote me a prescription for an antibiotic and had the nurse give me a starting dose. Dr. B always took care of us. We loved him.

Amy had always been healthy, other than chickenpox when she was two years old and occasional sore throats. One evening at home, I was surprised to realize my daughter had trouble breathing. Panicking, I brought her to the emergency center.

Dr. B. was on duty. He listened to her lungs, examined her ears and throat, and ordered a breathing treatment for her.

Watching your child struggle for breath is scary. I paced the hallway, trying to think positive. I hadn't fully appreciated what parents of asthmatics go through, even though the brother of a high school girlfriend of mine had died of an asthmatic attack years before. That thought occupied my mind as I watched my daughter gasping for air.

Amy was not asthmatic. Allergies must have triggered this attack. The breathing treatment worked. Her respiration rate began to normalize. Her struggle for oxygen subsided. I finally relaxed. Dr. B didn't charge for his treatment. Once again he'd taken care of us.

While I worked with Dr. B another afternoon, a frantic man rushed in with his wife in a wheelchair. "Help! My wife is having a baby!"

We got her back to the code room and on a bed just in time. Excited, our x-ray tech wanted to assist with the birth. She didn't have any children and the process fascinated her. Personally, I could've lived forever without seeing it, having had a difficult delivery years before myself. As a tiny twenty-year-old, I had given birth to a nine and one-half pound baby. The doctor who delivered Amy told me later that she had gotten stuck. He was just going to break her shoulders to get her out when I finally succeeded. Didn't care to remember the actual delivery, thank you anyway.

After she was born however, those days in the hospital after my only child joined me in the world proved to be the happiest days of my life. I still deeply resented anyone who tried to pressure me into giving my child up for adoption. That resentment would never go away.

So at work, I happily stepped aside to handle the steady stream of the other patients who came into the emergency center. Our new mother just a few feet away kept Dr. B, the nurse, and the x-ray tech busy. Dr. B stayed cool and calm as if he did this every day of his life, and delivered a healthy baby boy.

Then he turned his attention to the many other patients waiting. Hours later when all had quieted down, he went back to the doctor's room, sat at his desk, spread tobacco leaves on the desktop and rolled himself a cigar. Then he enjoyed a well-deserved smoke. Later, he bought us all dinner. So typical of his generosity.

A different afternoon, we had only one patient—an overweight male in his sixties.

"I'll need a CBC, UA, and Chemistry Panel," Dr. B said before retiring to the doctor's room to wait for results.

"I'm on it." Feeling needed and a valuable part of the medical team, I gathered my paraphernalia and approached the man to draw his blood for analyzing. Fat pads covered his arms, obscuring the veins lying deep below. I palpated for a vein but felt nothing. I searched the left arm—nothing. Right arm—nothing. Back of both hands—nothing. I took a deep breath and shook my head. This was going to be a challenge.

"They usually have to stick me a bunch of times," the patient said.

I believe it. Pulling up a stool to give my back a rest, I smiled and resumed my search. I would need two tubes, one for the CBC and a second one for the Chemistry Panel which included glucose, two kidney tests—BUN and creatinine—and electrolytes—sodium, potassium, chloride, and carbon dioxide. In frustration, I continued my search. He had to have a vein somewhere!

Wait! What was that? A thin ribbon deep below the surface. It was all I had. I had to go for it. I said a prayer and plunged the needle deep into the man's arm, then pushed the vacutainer through the back of the needle and held my breath.

Bingo! Pay dirt. I couldn't believe my luck. First try and I got it.

"Wow," the man said, "nobody's ever gotten me on the first try."

Oh, I'd had my share of misses in the past. Everyone gets lucky sometimes. With a sigh of relief I rushed back to the lab. Made the slide. Spun the clotted tube in the centrifuge to retrieve serum for the Chemistry Panel. We only had semi-automated machines so I manually diluted the tube for the white cell count, spun the hematocrit, and separately ran the hemoglobin.

"Here's the urine," our nurse said, popping into the lab with the urine sample she had collected for me.

"Thanks." If everything registered normal on the dipstick, no microscopic test would be required. But the dipstick showed abnormal readings so I spun the urine in the centrifuge. While that was spinning, I ran the Chemistry Panel on the serum. Nothing was simple with this patient. Laboratory procedure stated abnormal results needed to be repeated. Everything on this guy was abnormal. Instead of a numerical value on the glucose, the machine printed out "code 743." We hadn't had this particular machine very long and I wasn't used to the codes yet, so I grabbed the handbook down from the shelf and flipped through the pages to find the list of codes. Code 743—results out of range. Too low? Too high? I didn't know, so I grabbed a pipette and diluted the serum by two and re-ran.

Then the potassium printed out, with a result that was abnormally low. That, too, needed to be re-run in case it had short-sampled.

Meanwhile, the blood on the differential slide had dried so I could stain it. When I finished reading the slide, I shoved my chair away from the microscope, only to find another code had printed out on the Chemistry Panel machine. "Code 556." Now what?

I scanned the codes. 556—plugged needle or tubing. Oh, great. Suppressing a scream, I grabbed the flow chart of instructions to determine the problem and correct it. I zipped through the steps on the flow chart, quickly performing everything it suggested then ran the test-run per instructions on the chart.

Yes! Working now. A miracle. I immediately ran the patient's diluted glucose sample and re-ran the low potassium again.

Flying around the lab, I wrote my results onto the requisition slip, feeling good that I had resolved the multiple problems so quickly. I felt like I had performed miracles to solve the problems to present accurate results to the doctor as fast as humanly possible.

The glucose results printed out. Multiplying by the dilution factor for the high result, I was one minute from finishing everything when a deep voice boomed behind me.

"What's taking lab so long?" Dr. B came into the lab.

I stood in the middle of the room, requisition slip in my hand and stared at him, blinking my eyes in amazement. The list of problems with this patient flashed through my head. He had no veins but I got him! I had to troubleshoot the machine. I dealt with abnormal readings. I can guarantee my results are correct.

"Uh, here," I said and handed him the blood results and also my results of the urinalysis. "I had some trouble with the machine."

He nodded. "Oh. I thought maybe you'd fallen in."

Fallen in? I stared at him, incredulous, as he walked back to the patient. I've never known lab to get credit for solving lab problems. *Dr. B, if you weren't like an uncle to me, I'd throw something.* But I knew he was joking so I laughed. I could never stay upset with Dr. B. Who could? We loved him too much.

The patient turned out to be diabetic, and his water pill had caused a low potassium value. Dr. B and the nurse took care of him and then released him. We had all worked together to diagnose and treat this man.

At Christmastime, Dr. B threw a party at his home. He hired a piano player who played upbeat Christmas songs and other tunes. Tables of scrumptious food served the many guests. His home was large and beautifully decorated. People brought wine and toasted each other. He knew how to throw a party. A Navy-trained doctor, he was a good-old-guy.

I always looked forward to working with Dr. B. He was in his sixties but never wanted to retire. He loved being a doctor and helping people. He wanted to work forever. It gave him joy.

Later, all the employees of the emergency centers and the main hospital's ER were crushed by the news of his pancreatic cancer. He only lived three months after the diagnosis.

I still miss him and hope to run into him someday in that big Emergency Room in the sky. I picture him rolling his cigars, having a smoke, and helping the angels with any damaged wings they might have. It wouldn't be heaven for Dr. B. if he couldn't be helping someone.

Whenever I think of him, I smile toward heaven and nod my head. "Thanks, Dr. B. We love you. It was a privilege knowing you."

***

Over the years, I've done CPR on near-dead people, worked with gastric juices and fecal material, assisted with bone marrow aspirations, seen bones sticking out of flesh, etc. There are only a few things that make me woozy.

Holding a patient's eyelids open while the doctor drills—yes, drills—the rust out of the pupil is one. While the patient is awake!

Working with a patient's hands is another. I don't know why, but seeing the flesh and bones of someone's hand laid open is difficult for me.

One busy evening, patients filled every bed. A man lay in bed four with a hand injury. He had cut himself while working with equipment in his garage. The injury involved tendons so we called a hand surgeon for the repair. When the specialist arrived, I was the only staff member available to assist. Our x-ray tech had x-rays to do on another patient. The nurse had an IV to start on a different patient. Looked like I got the job to assist with the hand.

After preparing the sterile tray for the specialist whom I'd never met before, and opening the separate packs of sterile instruments he requested, I pulled a stool next to the bedside to help. The surgeon pulled the flaps of skin apart on the patient's palm and clasped them with forceps. "I'll need you to hold these flaps open for me while I work."

With my sterile gloves, I grasped a forceps in each hand and pulled the flaps open, revealing the inner workings of the hand beneath the palm's skin. The surgeon worked quickly and deftly. I was impressed with his skill. I had to ensure the flaps of skin always stayed out of his way while he worked, which forced me to watch his every move.

A white piece of stringy material had been cut—the tendon. Two pieces of tendon lay inside the patient's palm. The surgeon grasped one end of the tendon first and then the other end. The man's finger jerked as the tendon was pulled.

That's when I started to get woozy. *You can't faint. You're the only one available. Everybody else is busy. You have to keep it together.* But every time the surgeon pulled on the white tendon, the finger moved. Sweat began to form on my brow and drip down the side of my face. Nausea began to make its way up from my stomach to my throat. Things began to look blurry.

Yank—the finger jerked again. The surgeon moved quickly, pulling the severed tendon together and finally tying it into the tiniest knot I had ever seen. Fascinating. Snip, snip, the sound of metal against metal breezed toward me from a long distance away.

"Are you okay?" The doctor's voice floated through a misty fog.

Did my face look pale? How did he know? I had to be honest. "Well, sort of."

He knew we were busy. He knew I was the only one available to help him. He spoke in a soft and soothing voice. "You're doing great. I'm almost done. You're fine. I appreciate the good job you're doing." He continued to talk me out of my wooziness.

Gradually, the nausea subsided and the room stopped spinning. Objects became clearer. The doctor's hands moved swiftly as he finished the surgery, dabbing the blood and stitching the flaps. I could let go now. My part was over. I did it. I hadn't fainted. I felt better. I stood and retrieved the wraps and metal splint the doctor required to bandage the hand.

What a great doctor! Having to talk his assistant out of fainting while at the same time performing delicate surgery.

Amazing.

Once again, I felt proud of being a part of the medical field. Helping people. Watching the skill of other professionals at work. Many doctors amazed me with their knowledge. Nurses astounded me with their skills. X-ray techs impressed me. And I knew I, too, had special skills as a lab tech. I loved learning other aspects of the medical profession. I never thought I'd be able to do some of the things I did on my job. Things like catheterizing patients, performing CPR on heart attack victims, administering breathing treatments, or giving tetanus shots. I began to amaze myself!

***

Amy graduated from college in 1992. Mike and I watched her receive her college diploma as I nearly burst with pride. She got a part-time job as a math specialist in an elementary school.

Amy was doing well. My father was not. He had suffered for seven years from prostate cancer. My sister and I in Arizona took care of him in the winters and my other siblings helped him in the summers in Minnesota. By August of 1993, we knew he was very sick and didn't have long to live. I purchased plane tickets to go to Minnesota to see him the end of that August.

While waiting to go to Minnesota, Mike and I played tennis one hot summer evening. Amy came along and sat on a bench next to my court to watch. I played women's doubles while Mike played on a different court.

In the middle of the match, I walked to the back line to serve. Suddenly I had a strange sensation. A sense of outer-world peace surrounded me then surged through my body, filling me and lifting me with a calm I had never known before. It was like what I would describe as an out-of-body experience, although I had never had one.

I called out to Amy, "Amy, what time is it?"

She looked at her watch. "A few minutes after nine."

I nodded then resumed playing.

When we got home that night at ten-thirty, the light on our answering machine blinked in the darkness. I pushed the play button. It was my brother-in-law in Minnesota, telling us that my father had passed away that night. "A couple minutes after eleven o'clock. Nine o'clock your time."

I knew my father had come to say good-bye before he exited this world.

I had to remind myself he was out of pain and for him, it was a blessing. We flew to Minnesota for the funeral. At the service, I sat in the front pew, unable to choke back the tears. I remembered how my father had been there for Amy and me when we needed him. I missed my Dad and knew I would be forever grateful to him. We also had a service in November in Arizona for the Arizona people who couldn't be in Minnesota.

Later, I wrote a short story about him as a tribute, how he patiently taught us six kids how to water-ski, how he built our summer lakeside cabin by himself, the way he worked endlessly for his family. The story sold to three different magazines. To this day I still have dreams about my Dad and still miss him. Along with my siblings, I began helping my widowed mother.

A few months later, Amy met a plumber her age and they began dating seriously. Dad never met him but at least my mother did. For years I had hoped Amy would get into a good relationship, a common desire for all parents for their children. It looked like this may have happened.

***

In August of 1994, a rumor spread through our three

emergency centers that our owner, Phoenix Desert Hospital, planned on closing us all down due to poor finances.

I panicked. Not only would I miss the people with whom I'd worked for almost thirteen years, but I'd grown used to working with patients all day as opposed to working inside a laboratory. I knew that once I transferred to Phoenix Desert Hospital, I'd spend most of my time in the lab. It would be a major adjustment. New co-workers, new machines to learn, new methods of testing to master, new hours. Phoenix Desert was a trauma center and I'd be dealing with the stress of life-and-death trauma every day.

But I needed the money and hoped the main lab actually had a place for me. I would just have to get used to the new place.

Administration called a meeting for everyone at the emergency centers on my day off. I drove in, dreading to hear what they had to say. Department heads from Phoenix Desert Hospital came over—the head of nursing, the head of the X-ray department, the chief tech of the lab, and an office administrator. We all crowded into a small room.

I tried not to grind my teeth as I waited, hoping they had perhaps changed their minds and decided to keep us open. Sweat formed on my forehead. I didn't know if it was from my nerves or the summer heat.

The nursing administrator stood, greeted us and finally said, "We'll be closed by November."

We employees all looked at each other. Every one of us looked sad. The tension in the room grew thicker with the announcement. I felt like my professional life just crumbled down around me. I'd worked at the centers for over twelve years and had climbed up the salary/vacation ladder. I didn't wish to start at the bottom somewhere else, if I could even find a position elsewhere.

The head nurse continued, "Phoenix Desert Hospital promises to try to pull all of you into the main hospital if you wish to remain with us."

Yes, I wished! What a relief. Days or evenings, any lab department, I didn't care. I just needed full-time hours.

We breathed a collective sigh of relief. Even though it would be an adjustment, at least we had jobs. After the meeting, the big boss of the main lab gathered with us in a cramped room at the emergency center, along with our immediate lab supervisor, the tech who worked there, and me.

Feeling reassured by the head nurse's words in the meeting, I asked, "So, what's available for us at the hospital?"

The lab's big boss turned to the other tech first. She'd been with Phoenix Desert Hospital one year longer than I had and therefore had seniority over me in the company. "We do have an available spot in hematology on day shift. You can have that shift if you'd like," he said to her.

A big smile burst onto her face. "Sure!"

I was glad for her. Then our boss turned and looked at me. What would he offer me? I tried my hardest to smile.

"I don't think there is anything for you." He looked straight at my face and didn't even flinch.

He may as well have slapped me. I stared at him, wordless, trying not to show my shock. My legs felt wobbly and I felt a little woozy. I grabbed the counter with one hand to steady myself. After years of working as a loyal employee and that's all he had to say to me?

"Well, I have to get back to the hospital now." He left. Evidently, without an ounce of concern for me. He'd known me for almost thirteen years, had hired me, and now all he could say to me was, "I don't think there is anything for you," without even blinking.

I stood there trying to absorb what had just happened. Jobs were tight. Mike had a steady job with a decent salary working for the state but not enough for a house payment, two car payments, putting into two retirement funds, paying off Amy's college bills and supporting all three of us. We needed my salary badly.

My immediate lab supervisor, who worked in the main hospital lab as evening shift supervisor under the direction of our big boss, said to me, "Don't worry. I'll find you something."

God bless him! What a sweetie. I resisted the urge to throw my arms around him and kiss him. I felt a little better and appreciated his sentiment, but if the big boss didn't approve of it and if there weren't any openings, was there anything the evening supervisor could possibly do? I thanked him and we all dispersed. I headed home.

My birthday came a few days later. I had to work that day. I didn't mind. We always celebrated each other's birthdays at work with cake and cards. It would be a good day with friends.

I arrived at work but no one said "Happy Birthday." Lunchtime came but no cake. I didn't see any cards. *Hmmm, they must be planning a surprise for later. Maybe this afternoon.* I patiently waited as we tended to patients throughout the day.

Then dinnertime came. Still nothing. Must be a surprise after dinner! But the x-ray tech went home at the end of her seven a.m. to seven p.m. shift, being on-call for the rest of the evening. Just the nurse, receptionist and I stayed with the doctor until closing at eleven p.m.

No surprises.

I drove home that night feeling depressed. My friends at work, who knew what the lab's big boss had said to me, forgot my birthday. Work really couldn't have gotten much worse.

The next day I had off and I slept late. At about eleven a.m., as I was finishing a cup of coffee, the doorbell rang. I opened the door and there stood a young man holding a bouquet of flowers. Forget-me-nots.

The card said, "Sorry we forgot your birthday. Have a happy day!" All my friends at work had signed it.

I closed the door and sat down, staring at the card and beautiful flowers. I was so touched I almost cried. Such sweethearts I worked with! Then I called them at work and thanked them.

Suddenly, life seemed better. Maybe everything would work out all right after all. I would go where God wanted me. But man, was I going to miss those women from the emergency centers.

That evening, I played tennis at a resort that was popular with my tennis group. Afterwards, we went into the lounge for happy hour and a cold beer. I stood in line for the buffet, loading my plate with samples of the various foods offered. Chips and Salsa. Tacitos. Mini-chimichangas and guacamole. The line moved slowly so I munched on chips and salsa while waiting.

Looking around the room, I recognized two men sitting in a booth—the head of personnel at Phoenix Desert Hospital and his assistant.

I wondered if I should go over and tell them what my chief

tech said to me the previous day. I had nothing to lose. Perhaps I could appeal my case to them.

Nervous about approaching them and what the outcome might be, I munched on more chips and salsa as I debated whether I should talk to them or not. My personality tended toward the shy side. I watched the two men as they looked around, checking out the chicks.

I knew I looked good in my tennis outfit—black short skirt and white top. They were both single guys, I knew. That should work to my advantage, even if I was married. Should I do it? Did I dare? I wished I weren't so shy, but if a lady doesn't stick up for herself, she has no one to blame but herself, I told myself.

I worked my way through the buffet line and then purposely walked toward their table on my way back to my seat on the other side of the room. My hopes soaring and my heart flying, I stopped at their table. "Excuse me, don't you two work at Phoenix Desert Hospital?" I smiled my sweetest smile, feigning ignorance.

They both looked up at me, surprised. "Why, yes, we do."

"I thought I recognized you." My voice dripped with honey. I was beginning to nauseate myself, but they seemed to like it. "I work in the lab at the emergency centers."

"Oh, they're closing in a while, aren't they?" the personnel manager said.

"Yes. We had our meeting a few days ago and they formally announced the closing."

"What are you going to do? Work at the main lab?"

Here's my chance! I took a deep breath. "Well, I'd love to. I need the job. But our chief tech told me at the meeting that he didn't have anything for me."

"How long have you worked there?"

"Almost thirteen years."

His eyes narrowed and a flash of anger crossed his face. "Phoenix Desert Hospital doesn't operate that way." His voice lowered and he spoke slowly, enunciating each word. "That man doesn't do what he wants to do. He does what we tell him to do!"

Whew! I felt so relieved that my face burst into a huge grin. "Thank you! I feel much better now."

"Don't worry. You'll have a place. If you have a problem, just call me."

167

I thanked them both and practically bounced across the room and sat down in my seat. I did it! Victory was mine. I felt smart and clever and cute in my tennis outfit, all at the same time. I sighed with pleasure, so proud of myself. Now I had some leverage.

Then I glanced down and suppressed a scream.

There was a big blob of salsa sitting on my left breast.

Amy's cousin, Amy, my sister Kathie, another cousin on the infamous trip through the desert to Tucson's Desert Museum

Amy, Mickey, and me at Disneyland

Amy and me

Two cousins, Amy and my sister Ann at the lake in MN

Me and Mike

PART FOUR
TRAUMA CENTER

That September of 1994, the lab's big boss told me, "We have a two day per week position available in the chemistry department if you're interested."

Better than nothing. It was a start. Chemistry was my favorite department and I had experience performing chemistry tests.

The Emergency Centers didn't close down until November. This gave me two more months. I trained part-time in chemistry at the hospital while I continued working twelve hour shifts in the centers. Two days a week I got out of bed at 4:30 a.m. and worked in chemistry from 6:00 a.m. to 2:30 p.m. Two other days a week I worked 11:00 a.m. to 11:00 p.m. at the emergency center, getting home at 11:30 p.m. and asleep by 12:30. I constantly battled the adjustment. I was in my forties now and felt like I was starting all over.

I had to learn the layout of the hospital, how to process the samples, and operate the various machines in that particular lab because there are hundreds of different methods and machines in the world. Also, Phoenix Desert Hospital was computerized, making it necessary for me to learn many computer codes. I had never worked in a computerized lab before. All of this plunged me into a whole different working world.

My first day there, the head of chemistry asked me, "Have you even ever worked in a hospital chemistry lab before?" Her voice held no warmth.

"Yes, but it was years ago in the late seventies, and it wasn't computerized."

She didn't smile.

Not one of the day shift chemistry techs, all women, appreciated the many skills I had developed over the last sixteen years of my entire medical career. They all looked at me with distrust. The turnover in that lab was very low and they weren't used to many new people. My stomach ached.

Another chemistry tech, Isabelle, acted particularly rude to me, always giving me dirty looks. Never explained anything to me. Walked away from me in a huff. I feared asking her anything.

The air in that department reeked with tension. It was obvious they didn't take to new people disrupting their daily routine. I tried to see things from their point of view. They were happy with the way things were and the hospital suddenly thrust me upon them. No one in chemistry had ever met me before and they knew nothing about me. I could understand their reluctance to accept a new person into their group, but didn't they need another part-timer?

Their need for another chemistry tech, and their negative reaction to a new person, confused me. My head throbbed every day.

Just to make matters worse, in case things weren't bad enough, I started noticing words and numbers getting smaller and smaller. I got glasses and it took a few days for my vision to adjust to the progressive lenses. It took time to see my test results while my eyes searched up and down for that small window where I could see. Isabelle had no patience with me. She wanted instant feedback from me.

My varied hours, switching back and forth between the emergency center and the main hospital, adjusting to wearing glasses for the first time in my life, dealing with women who weren't exactly welcoming me with open arms, learning new machines and computer chemistry codes, all rattled my nerves and twisted my stomach. I had trouble sleeping at night, fighting back tears.

The two days a week I walked through the door of the emergency center, pure heaven awaited me. How would I ever adjust to working in that hospital?

I felt jerked back and forth. One day heaven and familiar surroundings, the next day tension in the main hospital lab. "Stat!" the lab aides called out all day long as they dropped sample after sample off in the hospital lab.

"Blue Alert. ETA three minutes!" blared over the hospital's

intercom. As a trauma hospital, they had blue alerts throughout each day. Blue Alerts took precedence over everything else of course, since they were life or death situations where seconds counted. My heart hammered with fear and my palms sweated every time I heard that announcement as I tried to remember the Blue Alert protocol. I couldn't afford to be slow or do anything wrong.

"Stat!" the lab aide said again with a different blood sample.

"Here's the Blue Alert." The aide placed the precious samples into the test tube rack. Everyone rushed around. Stress crackled in the air. But this was what I had trained for and I enjoyed the work itself. It'll get better, I thought, forcing myself to keep calm.

One morning, the announcement, "Full code, cardiac unit," came over the hospital intercom.

Just then the head of chemistry said to me, "Why don't you take your morning break? It's time."

Break? Take a break when there was work to be done? After running a one-person lab for years, the concept of a break with work to be done didn't occur to me. But I joined some other techs in the break room and plopped down with a much needed cup of coffee and tried to shake the stress off my shoulders for fifteen minutes.

When I returned from break, the other two chemistry techs on duty, Isabelle and the chemistry supervisor, took their break, leaving me alone in the department.

"Chemistry. Line Two," the front office called.

I picked up the phone.

A woman's harried voice came across the line. "This is the cardiac unit. We have a full code up here. Anthony Wilson. I need to know what his CPK read on his profile this morning." A CPK is a blood test for heart enzymes.

Isabelle had responsibility for CPK's that day. I hadn't been trained in that particular area of chemistry yet and didn't have a clue how to get into that particular machine's computer to retrieve the CPK results that hadn't been reported yet.

Dozens and dozens and dozens of samples had to be processed throughout the morning and it was only nine a.m. I went to the break room and told Isabelle, "CCU needs the CPK on Anthony Wilson from this morning. He's coding."

To my shock, Isabelle laughed. "Oh, that's Dr. Martinez. He knows me."

So? I waited but she just sat there. "They need Wilson's CPK result."

"Just tell them I'm on my break and I'll call them back."

Excuse me? I wasn't used to this attitude. In the emergency center, we jumped when the doctor needed a result. After years of working side by side with doctors and nurses, I had finally come to feel integrated into their team. Was Isabelle that far removed from the patient and the concept of teamwork? I felt like I had skidded backwards sixteen years in time when I started my lab career and at first felt disconnected with patients.

No way in hell was I going to tell that nurse she'd have to wait for the lab tech to finish her coffee to get the result on her coding, dying patient.

"He's coding. Right now!" I said.

She laughed again. "Oh, just tell Dr. Martinez that it's Isabelle. He's my doctor."

Who the hell did she think she was? I wasn't about to get yelled at by some nurse for the sake of Isabelle. I felt a strong duty to help out that doctor and nurse. So I went to Isabelle's station and waded through the papers, hoping it was done. Found it! Done but not reported in the computer.

This could mean any number of things. Was it a valid result? Had the QC been okay for the morning run? Had the blind duplicate QC passed? Was there a plug in the needle? Had the machine short-sampled? Had she diluted the sample first? Any number of things could have gone wrong. I had no idea if that result was correct or not. It was Isabelle's responsibility to analyze the validity of that number printed on a piece of paper.

On the other hand, I saw no troubleshooting code listed next to the result—nothing on the printout to indicate a problem existed. No notation anywhere indicating the sample had been diluted which would require a multiplication factor. Probably not, since it was the first run of the day. Even though I'd never been on that machine before in my life, I had enough experience to know what to look for.

The phone's red light blinked at me. Screw Isabelle. Screw this lab. I felt a duty to the patient, the doctor and the nurses trying to save him. I picked up the phone and gave the nurse the result.

I never heard anything else about it. And I never heard if Mr. Wilson made it or not. But I sure felt better.

***

November came too quickly. I worked at the Emergency Center the last day of its existence. In between patients, my co-workers and I helped pack. At eleven p.m. we quietly turned off the lights, swiped out, set the alarm, locked the doors, and walked to our cars for the last time.

"Good night," we called to each other. Sadness squeezed my heart. Almost thirteen years of my life in that scenario now became my past. Slowly, we all drove our separate ways.

The main hospital trauma lab now became my life. One afternoon the next week I looked at the clock on the chemistry department's wall—two o'clock. Just another half-hour before my shift ended.

The big boss came over to me as I worked on the SMAC 20 machine. "I need to talk to you about something. Can you come by my office when your shift is over?"

I nodded, afraid he planned to tell me he had no other hours for me except the sixteen hours a week in chemistry. We could never live on that. I'd been praying he'd find more hours for me. With Amy's college bills to pay, with her just working part-time, and my car had just broken down, we needed the money.

At two-thirty I swiped out and went to his office to find his door closed. *That's odd. His door is never closed.* I decided to run to the ladies room and then come back.

When I returned, his door stood open. I said another quick prayer, stepped in and sat down in the small room, my heart fluttering wildly.

He shook his head as he sat behind his desk which took most of the space. "This is hard to believe. When I went to you at two o'clock and asked you to come here and talk to me, I planned to tell you all I had to offer you was a part-time graveyard shift. You'd be replacing the person with the least amount of seniority in the lab."

So that was it. I would work two days a week 6:00 a.m. to 2:30 p.m., and three days a week 11:00 p.m. to 7:00 a.m. A crazy schedule for sleeping. And I was costing someone their job. What a nightmare, on so many levels.

Over the many years I had worked in a medical lab, I worked dayshift, evenings, graveyards, and nights with being on-call over the graveyard shift. I had no desire to work graveyards again. Been there, done that. Especially when after one day off, I would have to flip to an early morning day shift. My insides felt like they were being pulled through an old washing machine wringer. I needed the job and didn't seem to have much choice but how long could I last in that nightmare? I wasn't getting any younger. Twenty years prior, I could have possibly handled that schedule. But definitely not now at my age. An elephant pressed down on my shoulders, making it difficult to breathe.

Before I could respond, he continued. "Then just a few minutes ago, Rachel came to my office." Rachel was a tech who worked part-time evening shift. "She had evidently applied at a private lab for a management position. They called her at two-fifteen today and offered her the job. She gave me her resignation just a few minutes ago. So now I can offer you a part-time evening shift."

Hallelujah! Praise the Lord! I could handle that. Once I moved over to the main lab I would work two shifts a week in the days and three shifts a week on evenings. Not bad.

He shook his head again. "I can't believe the timing of that phone call. It's incredible."

It wasn't incredible to me. I smiled. "Not so hard to believe. I've been praying and God answered my prayer." And just in the nick of time! Our big boss was a Catholic and surely would appreciate that, I figured.

To my surprise, he looked irritated. "Well, whatever. Are you interested in the job?"

A strange reaction from him, but I answered, "Sure!" The elephant jumped off my shoulders and I breathed deeply. I knew I would enjoy evenings. I already knew some of the people on evenings and they were very friendly.

On evenings, I would be working blood gases, hematology, coagulation, and a little bit of microbiology. I had experience in all those departments but their machines and methods were completely different. And of course there were the computer codes to learn for each department. Those topics interested me and I looked forward to working evenings.

For a while, I trained three day shifts a week in hematology while working my two days a week in chemistry. I was still a little bit slow in chemistry but gaining speed each day. Most of the other chemistry techs worked only in the chemistry department, had been there for years, and had nothing other than chemistry to worry about. Of course they were faster than me! But they had no patience with my slowness. I'd like to see them do what I had to do!

At this time I learned the reason behind their coldness to me. There had been another tech in chemistry whom they all liked but she had only been at Phoenix Desert Hospital a couple years. Since I had experience in chemistry and only minimal experience in microbiology, our big boss moved her into an open microbiology position and me into her part-time chemistry position. The chemistry women resented losing the tech they liked and were stuck with someone they didn't know.

So that explained it. I felt a little better, realizing it hadn't been personal, but they needed to get used to it. Too bad, ladies. Not my fault. I had been an employee of that hospital for almost thirteen years. They owed me. The hospital promised us when they closed the emergency centers they would absorb all of us. I was getting tired of the cold shoulder treatment. At least nobody had lost their job now because of me. I couldn't imagine how much worse it would've been for me if that had happened.

I thanked God and soldiered on.

***

We had the sweetest dog—our beloved big black lab named Pepper. She loved to cuddle. She was protective of all of us. When we took walks, she stopped to smell the flowers, always reminding me to do the same. She'd bring her bone and lay it at my feet. Wouldn't everybody want that treasure?

Amy told me of a dream she had. Snakes covered the floor of her bedroom, squirming and wiggling. Frightened, she ran into the living room looking for me. "Help me," she screamed.

But I didn't get up. Instead, I calmly handed her a gun. "Here, use this," I said.

Angry that I wouldn't go with her, she grabbed the gun and ran to her bedroom. The snakes came toward her hissing and coiling to strike. She pointed the gun and fired. Water streamed out instead of bullets. As soon as the water touched each snake, the reptile turned into Pepper. Soon, dozens of Peppers filled her room, wagging their tails with joy.

A woman I knew who had written a book about dream interpretations analyzed this dream for me. "The snakes represent problems in Amy's life. Her initial instinct was to run to her mother to help her solve these perplexing issues. But because she's growing up, you didn't solve her problems for her. Instead, you gave her the tools she needed to solve this troubling situation herself. Then once she confronted the issue, the problems turned into Pepper, indicating the problems weren't as bad as she thought they were."

After that dream, whenever Amy was upset about something in her life, I'd say, "Now is this a snake, or a Pepper?" She learned she had what it took to navigate through life, turning negative situations into positive ones.

I thought of her childhood. The years had passed too quickly. One birthday party after another. I remembered a feeling of despondency had hung over me at the thought of her growing up and one day leaving me. But pride always filled me as I watched her mature.

Years ago, a nice boy had asked her to the prom. I took her to the JC Penney outlet store and we found a lovely blue dress we could afford.

I liked her friends. She found a nice group of girls to hang around with. Even the boys in her group were nice.

She had spent a week in California some summers for church camp. During the school year, she got an after-school job at a daycare center.

She had even taken up tennis for a while. My motto on the court was, "Better to be the stomper than the stompee." Amy's motto was, "It's nice when everyone gets a point."

I felt like I had missed a lot of her growing up while I worked crazy hours, weekends, holidays, evenings, nights. And then she got her driver's license and a job. I wished I could push a button and turn back time—grab onto and hold those precious hours of her childhood in a treasure chest where I could pull them out whenever I wanted to and relive them. But the natural order of Mother Nature didn't allow that.

***

In preparation for working evenings, I trained during the day in the hematology and coagulation departments both. I had briefly met the dayshift hematology supervisor several times over the past twelve years and liked her.

Hematology's main machine proved to be complex and all the computer codes in that department were different from the chemistry department's codes, intimidating me.

Trying not to show how nervous I felt, I sat in front of the big machine and hematology's supervisor sat next to me. "When a result is out of normal range, you need to highlight it," she said, handing me a yellow highlighter.

So I did.

Her face scrunched up into a vile look. She gritted her teeth.

What's going on? What did I do?

Her face burned red. She twisted her hands into fists. "You don't hold the highlighter that way! You hold it THIS way." She grabbed the highlighter out of my hand.

I blinked and stared at her, taken aback by her anger. What? Where did that come from? I'm holding the highlighter wrong? Is she kidding? How ridiculous. And so, another nightmare began. I couldn't do anything right in her eyes. It hurt my feelings because previously I'd liked her and thought she'd liked me. I didn't know why she was acting that way toward me. What had I gotten myself into? If jobs hadn't been so scarce and I needed the money so badly, I would've quit—or at least just stayed part-time in chemistry. But financial necessity forced me to stay.

Had the power of becoming a department supervisor gone to her head? She was a different person from the woman I had briefly known the past twelve years.

Day after day she towered over me, staring at and criticizing my every move. She made me so nervous I couldn't think straight, which didn't help matters because there was so much to learn before I moved to evenings. If she had asked me, "What is your name?" I don't think I could've answered correctly.

My mind couldn't come up with the names of the parts of a microscope. I'm sure I came off as an ignoramus at times. I didn't know if I could continue in that atmosphere. I had loved working in the medical field up until then but was now having second thoughts.

During a break one morning, I overheard her talking to some other techs. "I told Oliver I like the dress I bought for my sister's wedding. I think he likes it, too." "I discussed getting a new car with Oliver. We agreed I need a new one. So we're going together this weekend to look for one." "I was very upset about that incident at church last week. I talked to Oliver about it..."

I wondered who Oliver was. I knew she wasn't married. Maybe he was her brother. I hoped he was her boyfriend because if she was happy in a relationship, maybe that would eventually mellow her a bit. Later, I asked one of the other techs in the lab, "Who's Oliver?"

"Oh, he's one of her dogs."

It took me a moment to absorb this. Then I thought, *My God, what kind of a person was I working for?*

Another day, as I worked at the hematology back-up machine, her assistant, whom I'd just met, shouted across the small room to me, "You can't run that patient sample until you've run a control!" She stood there fuming, her teeth clenched, her body literally shaking.

Oh great, now even her assistant is jumping into the fray. That little area reeked with tension. I held up a half-empty vial. "I did already, see? It's just fine." My voice projected defiance. I wasn't going to take any crap from her.

Her lip curled into a sneer. She turned her back to me.

I had a lot to learn but they didn't have to be so vindictive. Employees in that lab had all been there for years and they weren't used to new people, I guess. It was like they lived in their own little castle and didn't want any changes. The hospital had forced me onto them and they obviously didn't like it. Did they know someone else they wanted to hire, I wondered.

I went home many nights crying. I called my fellow

emergency center lab tech to talk to her. She had completed her hematology training in the main lab already. I needed commiseration.

"At first I went home every night crying, too," she consoled me. "But it gets better. You just started in that department. Hang in there."

My shoulders relaxed. I don't know what I would have done without her. A fellow sufferer. I didn't feel so alone now and that helped. I thought about how things had gotten so much better in chemistry in just the three months I had worked there. I actually liked the people in chemistry now, something I never thought would happen. Things would get better as soon as I finished training in hematology. Then when I finished training in coagulation and blood gases for Blue Alerts, I could switch to evenings. I liked the evening shift people and could not wait to get away from the hematology day shift.

To my surprise, my two shifts a week in the chemistry department became my refuge now. The people there had finally accepted me. I was getting faster and more organized and felt at ease with the work and my co-workers. I respected their skills. They were actually friendly to me—not such bad people after all. We ate lunch together, went to break together, talked and got to know each other personally. Isabelle loved my hair and convinced me to grow it longer. We all discussed good books we had read, movies to see or avoid, television shows we liked, trips we planned to take. The desert's winter weather was gorgeous and some of us took quick walks together after lunch before returning to the windowless lab. I filled in for them when they took days off, which they appreciated.

Finally I moved to evening shifts for my other three shifts a week. Good-bye, hematology supervisor. And her irritable assistant. And Oliver.

The people on evenings didn't criticize my every move, and even helped me if I had a problem. Thank God. No day shift administration looked over my shoulder anymore. What a relief. It wasn't long before I felt part of the evening team and was able to help them out in return. My nervousness and fear abated as time went by and I began to enjoy working in the hospital lab.

We covered for each other on our breaks, bonded on busy

nights as we all scrambled and experienced the same tension, and when it wasn't busy we talked and shared treats we brought in to eat. Sometimes we went out for a cocktail after our shift ended at eleven p.m.

I found the work intellectually stimulating and rewarding and became friends with the other techs. In December, the chemistry department met at a restaurant for dinner and a fun gift exchange and the evening shift met for lunch. All my co-workers had accepted me and I didn't have to deal with day-shift hematology at all. I never got used to those two women in hematology. The transition was complete and I could finally say, once more, "I love my job."

***

"Blue Alert. ETA two minutes." The announcement blared over the hospital's intercom system.

My first Blue Alert alone. It was evening and we were a small group, just three of us techs and an aide for the entire lab. Blue Alerts took precedence over everything else since they were life and death situations. I was assigned to blood gases and hematology that night, which meant I was the one who had to go to the Blue Alert to draw the arterial blood for the blood gas. I grabbed my tray and raced down to the ER. The seriousness of the situation made me nervous.

After donning a blue paper hair cover, a mask, paper gown, blue paper booties over my shoes, and gloves, I tried to get to the patient. People crowded into the room—a trauma doctor, the ER doctor, multiple nurses each with their own specific duties, a lab aide for the venous blood, and two x-ray techs. Everyone rushed around in a well-synchronized madhouse. I elbowed my way through the throng to the patient who thrashed around on the bed. Head injury? Drunk? I didn't know.

A nurse standing next to me tried to start an IV but was unable to, due to the patient's frantic movement. After years of helping nurses and nurses helping me in the emergency centers, I didn't hesitate for a second. I put my syringe, betadine swab, gauze, and elastic wrap down on the bed and held the patient's flailing arm for the nurse so she could get the IV started.

When she finished, I collected my paraphernalia in two seconds and turned to the patient to draw the blood gas. But the nurse was gone. I looked around but couldn't find her. She'd disappeared into the crowd of medical personnel.

What the heck? I'd assumed she'd return the favor and help me. Gee, thanks a lot! I grabbed the patient's thrashing arm and could barely hold it still. How could I ever get a needle into the artery this way? It was like trying to maneuver thread through the eye of a moving, jerking needle.

"Did you get the blood gas yet?" An angry voice sounded next to me.

I looked up to see the ER doctor staring at me. I recognized her. She was the emergency center doctor years ago, back when I didn't know how to strap a child into a papoose board. I'm sure she didn't recognize me after all this time, especially because a mask covered my face and my hair was covered.

"Uh, no, I haven't."

Black anger blazed in her eyes and she screamed, "Well, MOVE IT! MOVE IT! MOVE IT!"

Startled, I jumped but had gone through too much the previous weeks and months to take this treatment lying down. Something inside me snapped. My words came out in a snarl, surprising even me. "I was helping the nurse start the IV but then she disappeared and didn't help me." Too much frustration boiled just beneath my usual professional demeanor for me to care about standing up to this doctor.

The doctor looked shocked at my outburst and walked away.

By God, I wasn't going to let some thrashing patient, probably drunk, get me into trouble. With my left hand, I gripped the patient's arm and held it tight. With my right hand, I swabbed the wrist clean, felt for a pulse, then yanked the cap off the needle with my teeth, said a prayer, plunged the needle in and breathed relief when bright red blood pumped into the syringe with every heartbeat. Thank you, Lord!

Ripping my mask off as I raced down the hall back to the lab with the precious sample, I realized I had learned a valuable lesson. Things were different here in the main hospital. Here, every man and woman scrambled for him/herself. No helping another department like we did back in the emergency centers. You do your own job yourself here and get out. Assisting someone else would just put me behind in my own work and get me yelled at. I never helped another nurse in a Blue Alert again.

***

Crossing the threshold into the laboratory at the beginning of my shift was sometimes like entering another world where mad activity didn't stop for the next eight hours. The place hummed with phones ringing, centrifuges whirring, the aides shrieking "STAT!" as they placed tubes of blood in a rack, beepers going off, and Blue Alert announcements blaring over the intercom.

Some people thrive on that excitement. Yes, I needed a challenge for a job to hold my interest and I loved the work itself, but the tension in a Trauma Center made me nervous. I hoped to get used to it in time.

One evening I donned my white lab coat, pulled on latex gloves, stocked my supplies, checked the machines I'd be working on, calibrated with standards, ran controls, checked for precision and accuracy, looked for shifts or trends, did the necessary paperwork, and readied myself for the night. I was covering blood gases, hematology, coagulation, and urinalysis. And whoever had time between the three of us evening techs would go into microbiology and plate specimens and read gram stains.

Specimens arrived at a steady pace. Plenty of work to keep me busy that evening. A lab aide walked back and handed me a requisition slip. "This just came down the vacuum tube from the nursery." It was an order for a routine capillary blood gas to be drawn at six p.m. on a newborn.

"Thanks." At ten minutes before six, I gathered my tray and wrote "nursery" on the white board to let my co-workers know where I was.

Just then my beeper went off. The ER needed a blood gas drawn. There's a hierarchy of importance of procedures. ER stats took precedence over routine nursery. I erased "nursery" from the board and wrote "ER" and left.

When I got to the ER, the unit clerk handed me three slips. "Three blood gases," she said, "but you need to go to Bed One first. I don't have the paperwork on her yet. I'll get it to you as soon as I get the information on her."

Four gases in all. I hurried to Bed One. An elderly woman, who looked about ninety, lay in bed. Her eyes stared lifelessly into space, unblinking. Her mouth hung open behind a clear oxygen mask. A male respiratory therapist stood at the head of the bed rhythmically squeezing an oxygen bag connected to the mask. The patient's legs curled up toward her body in a fetal position. Her skin was very pale with a light grey pallor. Wires connected her to a monitor next to the bed. My first thought was, *She looks dead.*

I readied my needle and syringe then felt for a radial pulse in her wrist. Nothing. Hmmm. I readjusted my fingers. Still nothing. I then moved up and felt inside her elbow for a brachial pulse. Nothing. I glanced at the readings on the monitor next to her. The number eighty displayed on the screen, indicating a normal pulse. But that wasn't possible!

"She doesn't have a pulse," I said to the respiratory therapist who squeezed the oxygen bag again, forcing the life-saving gas into the patient.

A harried-looking nurse rushed in, opened a drawer, and gathered some supplies.

The therapist looked at the monitor then gave me an indulgent smile. "Her pulse is eighty." He continued squeezing the oxygen bag, slowly and rhythmically, completely calm.

Irritated that he wouldn't believe me, I said, "It couldn't be."

The respiratory therapist repeated with authority, "Her pulse is eighty."

The busy nurse said, "The monitor hasn't been reset. Those are old readings." She then rushed out to care for another emergency patient.

The respiratory therapist and I looked at each other. A look of panic flashed across his face. "She doesn't have a pulse?"

I shook my head. "No," I insisted again.

He pulled in a deep breath. "FULL CODE! Bed One!"

Suddenly someone yanked the curtain back and shoved a crash cart into the tiny room. There was maybe a foot of space surrounding the bed and that was all. A crew of people swarmed into the tiny space.

I was in their way. I couldn't get an arterial gas anyway since she didn't have a pulse. The code team began working on the patient, trying to revive her.

I still had three blood gases to collect in the ER, plus the capillary blood gas in the nursery to collect, plus hematology and coagulation stats waiting for me in the lab, and I couldn't get Bed One's blood gas. A feeling of panic pushed its way up into my chest, throbbing higher and higher, threatening to overtake me. I was swamped. I mentally shoved the panic down to my stomach where I could possibly deal with it and tried to organize my thoughts. *I'll go do one of the other three patients then come back.* I didn't have time to waste a precious few minutes waiting for Bed One to be revived.

I went to another ER bed and collected a blood gas, labeled it, went to the ice machine, filled a cup with crushed ice, put the sample on ice, then hurried back to Bed One to see if the code team had revived that patient yet. The Code Team was still there so I went to draw a different patient.

In a couple minutes I returned to Bed One. Only one nurse, the respiratory therapist, and an ER doctor were left from the code team. They must have revived her. The doctor saw me enter and said, "Do you have the blood gas results yet?"

Results? Was he crazy? I gulped. "No, I haven't got the sample yet."

He looked at me as if I were the most incompetent human being on earth. "Give me the syringe," he said through gritted teeth. "If you can't handle it, I'll do it." He yanked it out of my hand, felt the patient's groin for a pulse and went deep into the groin with the needle, withdrawing bright red blood. He smiled and turned to the respiratory therapist who was still squeezing the oxygen bag and said, "Great job oxygenating."

The doctor then turned to me and thrust the syringe and needle toward me. "Here!" he said gruffly, "I want this STAT! Do you think you can manage that?"

I held my tongue and raced back to the lab. How ironic, I thought. The respiratory therapist thinks he's oxygenating a patient and I'm the one who has to tell him the patient's heart isn't even beating. All the oxygen in the world won't help if the heart isn't beating to circulate it. Yet it's the therapist who gets a compliment and I get a dirty look. Great. Just great.

I analyzed the three samples I had, then ran back to the ER to collect the other patient, rushed back to the lab to analyze it, then dashed up to the nursery to collect the capillary blood gas, then ran back to the lab to analyze it before trying to get caught up on the stat hematology and coagulation samples as more poured in.

While my stomach growled at me from lack of dinner, I sat at a microscope and examined a differential-slide. A woman dressed in a suit came into the lab, looked around and walked over to me.

"I'm the charge nurse for the hospital tonight," she said. She was dressed in street clothes. Her voice was soft and her demeanor friendly. "The ER doctor called me wanting me to find out why he isn't getting his differential-slide results faster."

Was that idiot doctor kidding? First he complains I didn't get a dead woman's blood gas fast enough, now he's complaining he's not getting microscopic results fast enough. I looked up at the woman and my mouth gaped open, unsure of how to word my response.

Just then the lab aide up front called back to me, "Nursery needs a stat blood gas drawn."

In the hierarchy of importance, nursery stat blood gases took precedence over ER stat differential-slides. I said, "I gotta go." She gave me a sympathetic look. I left the slide on the microscope stage, pushed back my chair, got up, grabbed my tray, wrote "nursery" on the board, and hurried out, tired and hungry.

Did that ER doctor think the whole lab was all in the lounge relaxing or something? Just having a fun time, chit chatting and laughing, ignoring our work? Evening shift was always a skeleton crew. None of us had eaten dinner yet that night.

The situation presented a common problem. If a tech complains he/she needs more help, that person might as well wear a sign blaring, "I'm not fast enough or good enough to handle my job." It became a point of pride to work a busy shift and keep up. If others didn't request extra help, I couldn't either, or it would've looked bad for me. Calling in the on-call tech to come in from home cost the lab a lot of money. I didn't want to cost the lab extra money, so I hurried even faster.

I assumed that nice charge nurse must have stuck up for me against the ER doctor's complaint because I never heard anything more about the delay in receiving the differential-slide results. That's all I would've needed—a complaint from a doctor. Bless that hospital charge nurse! And I got all the work done by the end of my shift.

***

In late November I ran into one of my favorite emergency center doctors, Dr. H., in the ER. I had acted in her safety video. We had gone out to lunch before and I told her I missed working with her.

Then one Saturday night in December, I was working again in blood gases and my beeper went off. I grabbed my tray and went down to the ER. It was seven p.m. which meant change of shift for the doctors.

Dr. H. walked in through the door, carrying a colorfully wrapped package. She brightened when she saw me. "I hoped to run into you," she said. She extended her arm, holding out the present. "This is for you."

"For me? What for?" Surprised, I took the package. There was no card.

"Just a Welcome to the Main Hospital gift. Glad to have you on board."

How thoughtful of her! I was deeply touched. "Thank you!" I hugged her.

I went into Bed Two to draw the blood gas, placing my gift on the counter behind the bed. The patient was a twenty-nine-year-old male stretched out as if asleep. The nurse entered the room for a minute to check on something, then left. I recognized her but didn't know her personally.

I inserted a needle into the patient's radial artery to withdraw the blood sample. He didn't flinch. When finished, I grabbed my tray and gift and returned to the lab.

A few minutes later, that same ER nurse marched into the lab. She stood in the middle of the room and looked around until she saw me. She trounced over to me where I was busy working. Her lips clenched together forming a thin line. Her eyes narrowed in an angry gaze.

What the heck? I had stats piled up in hematology and was concentrating on getting them done.

The nurse pointed to Dr. H.'s gift to me sitting on the

countertop next to me. "Whose present is that?" she demanded, her tone frosty on this cold December night.

"Mine. Why?"

"When you went into Bed Two there was a present on the counter. When you left, the present was gone. The patient was probably Christmas shopping for his wife or girlfriend." She stood with hands on hips and glared at me.

The bitch. Did she really think I stole it? "No, it's mine," I said in a firm tone.

"Where did you get it?"

"Dr. H. gave it to me. I saw her when I got to the ER."

"Why would she give you a present?"

Who did this woman think she was? I spoke slowly. "Because we're friends."

"Well, I think it belongs to the patient."

"No, it's mine," I repeated. I didn't have time to deal with this nonsense.

"Well, what's in it?"

"I don't know. I haven't opened it."

"Well, I want to see it."

These days I would have told her to shove it, but back then my personality was much meeker. I had planned on opening my present at home away from the craziness of work. But I just wanted to get rid of this woman. With no time to argue, I opened the package. It was a light scented room spray from France.

"Hunh," the nurse grunted. She didn't seem completely satisfied but what could she do? She whirled around and marched back out.

The evening chemistry tech walked over to me. "What was that all about?" She was a pretty woman and everybody liked her. She had become a friend of mine and looked concerned. I appreciated her support and told her what happened.

"I just did a drug screen on that guy," she said. "He was positive for four different drugs."

No wonder he was passed out. "And that nurse thought he was Christmas shopping tonight. Looks like he was busy doing something else!"

I tried not to take the incident personally. The nurse didn't know me at all. Rather, I thought it was a slam to the entire laboratory. Why would a professional medical technologist go to college for years, give up her Saturday night to work in a hospital, deal with drug addicts, needles, and Blue Alerts, just to steal some patient's little gift she saw on a countertop, thereby risking her job, license and career? It was insane. Didn't she think that lab personnel cared about patients? How insulting, as if she thought nurses were the only ones with professional ethics.

This differed so much from my experience at the emergency centers, where nurses and lab and x-ray all worked together as a team and respected each other. I tried to get this nurse out of my mind. It upset me too much. Piles of work waited for me.

***

One week before Christmas, all the chemistry techs met at a restaurant for an annual holiday dinner. A graveyard shift tech came in early to cover for the evening chemistry tech so she could join us. Everyone looked different in street clothes—a gathering of pretty women, relaxed and friendly. I had a fun evening. The evening shift also had an annual Christmas get-together. We met at a restaurant for lunch, everybody wearing their holiday sweaters. A great group of people.

I enjoyed talking with the evening shift crew when we went out for a drink after work. For years, I'd been a one-person lab at the centers and now I had other lab people to talk "lab talk" with. On our birthdays, we bought pies from Marie Callender's to celebrate. It was like having a new family.

***

The next summer, Mike, Amy and I flew to Minnesota to visit and stay at my family's lakeside cabin. My father built the cabin in the 1950s on a half-acre of lakeshore land. The breezes off the water provided welcome relief for the three of us escaping Arizona's relentless summer heat.

Anyone or everyone could be found at the cabin at any given time. People slept all over—on the couch, on foam pads spread out on the floor, in the open bedroom. We made it work. But it did make things difficult for marital privacy.

Sleeping late, drinking coffee in the screened-in porch while watching the morning sun sparkle on the water, talking, enjoying the cool air, listening to the news, eating lunch, then afternoons swimming and rafting before coming in to shower, making dinner and playing cards all evening made up our typical days. As Amy grew older, I saw her less and less since she spent more and more time with her friends. I really enjoyed time spent with my daughter at the lake. But Mike and I always kept our eyes open for any possibility of being alone.

While spending hours on a rubber raft in the lake one afternoon, Mike and I enjoyed the peaceful atmosphere. The sun shone brightly in a cloudless sky. When it got too warm, I rolled off the raft into the shocking cool water.

"Should we go in?" Mike asked. "We've been in the sun a long time."

I was loving the water too much and could've stayed out there all day. "We're used to Arizona sun. Minnesota sun isn't as strong. Besides, you have your baseball cap on." I talked him into staying in the water longer.

Lake gulls glided above us then swooped down to grab a fish. I leaned back, closed my eyes and smiled up at the sun.

We finally went ashore. Laughing, we ran across the grass to the cabin for a shower.

Mike stopped and tilted his head. "Notice anything?"

"What?"

"The cars are gone. And it's quiet."

I listened. He was right. No TV. No chatter. "Hello? Anybody home?"

Silence.

We found a note in the kitchen. Amy was off visiting with cousins. My sisters left to go shopping. The other men were golfing.

We looked at each other and laughed, both thinking the same thing. Time alone! A rare occurrence. No chance of interruption.

"You shower first," I said, "because you're so fast." Plus, it took longer for me to peel off my swimsuit which had a tendency to cling.

Two minutes later, I jumped into the shower and quickly washed off the lake water then wrapped a big towel around myself and joined him in the bedroom. There he stood awkwardly, both arms held out to the sides a few inches from his torso.

"Mike. You look kind of burned." I walked closer to him and squinted my eyes. Bright red skin covered his shoulders, torso, and arms.

"That's okay," he said. "I don't mind." What a trooper.

Perhaps it just looked worse than it really was.

"All right." I wrapped my arms around his neck and pressed against him. Couldn't wait.

He screamed.

"Omigosh! Did I hurt you?" I backed away in alarm.

He looked at me like one looks at a child who just asked, "Why is the sky blue?"

"Just a little, my dove." We could barely laugh at his attempt at humor.

I felt horrible. It was entirely my fault. I was the one who'd talked him into staying on the water all afternoon. I'd forgotten he always wore a shirt in Arizona. His skin had been white as Minnesota snow before I forced him to bake in the Minnesota sun. Why was I so pushy?

"I'll get you some cream. Or spray. Or something." I ran to the medicine cabinet and flung it open. Rummaging through the junk, I found some lidocaine spray for sunburns. Oh, good. I glanced at the expiration date. Oops. Expired five years ago. I'd have to try it anyway because it was all I could find. I didn't tell him it expired.

To my surprise, he said the spray gave him some relief.

"Let's try this again." He pulled me towards him. I touched his arm.

He howled.

We looked at each other as it slowly dawned on us we had ruined our opportunity. It was like being in a romantic comedy movie. We burst out laughing. What else could we do?

By the time he healed, it was time to return to Arizona. On our future visits, we made sure he used sunscreen on his precious white body.

As a working mother, I felt like I rarely saw Amy anymore. Her teen years had whizzed by. She was already a college graduate and young adult now. Mike and I flew her to New York for a great trip. I'd never been to New York before. The three of us visited the Statue of Liberty and saw a Broadway show, Miss Saigon, with front row seats, courtesy of Mike's twin brother and wife who lived there. Loved it. We couldn't thank them enough.

Unfortunately, vacations are never long enough and it was back to work in just a couple weeks.

***

One evening at work, our lab aide called out, "Stat blood gas in Recovery!"

I grabbed my tray and rushed upstairs to the recovery room. A groggy elderly man lay in a post-operative bed, attached to an IV pole and oxygen. A young male doctor and young pretty nurse attended the patient, frantic looks on both their faces.

The doctor looked up when I walked in. "Oh, good, lab's here. We need a gas. Stat! His oxygen readings are dropping fast! I may have to intubate." The doctor and nurse hurriedly gathered their supplies, ready to save this man's life.

I glanced at the oxygen meter reading: 85. 83. 80. All in a matter of seconds. A normal oxygen reading is in the upper nineties.

The patient didn't look like he was in respiratory distress to me. His color was pink. I felt his skin. It was cool and dry. His breathing didn't appear labored.

But the number kept dropping. No wonder the doctor was alarmed, ready to intubate and force oxygen into him.

The patient kept moving his arms as he struggled to awaken from the anesthesia. I felt his radial pulse at his wrist. Strong. I could easily draw a blood gas there. I got out my needle, syringe, gauze, alcohol wipes, and elastic wrap.

Then I noticed the small oximeter at the tip of the man's finger. As the man moved, his oximeter moved, millimeter by millimeter. It needed to sit squarely on the finger in order to yield an accurate reading. I positioned the oximeter correctly so it hugged his finger securely. Then I watched the readings on the meter standing next to the bedside: 85. 90. 95. 97, in just a matter of seconds.

The doctor glanced at the meter, then jerked his head to stare at me, speechless. His brows furrowed in a questioning manner. His eyes squinted as if trying to comprehend what was happening. His mouth formed an O.

"His oximeter slipped," I said. "I put it back on him."

The doctor laughed and I could tell he was embarrassed. His face turned a chagrined red. "Wow." He gave a disgusted snort. "That's awful. It takes *lab* to figure out what's going on." The nurse and doctor looked at each other and shook their heads in disbelief.

How insulting! I shrugged my shoulders. "Well, lab's part of the team you know."

That seemed to pacify him a bit. He smiled a weak smile.

"Do you still need the blood gas?" I asked.

"No, not now."

I packed my paraphernalia and turned to leave, feeling good.

"Thanks," the doctor said.

I smiled at him and nodded. Anytime.

***

"It's a full moon tonight. It'll be a crazy one!" a co-worker said one night. Suspicions ran deep in hospital emergency rooms. Full moons always brought hectic days. And she was right. Open-heart surgery called saying they needed some on-the-spot blood tests run. When they called, we didn't walk there—we ran. We didn't even use the elevator. Instead we zoomed up the stairs. This gave me good exercise and because I was on my feet all day, the pounds stayed off.

On my way up the staircase to open-heart-surgery, I ran into a nurse I knew. As I passed her, I said, "Up and down these stairs every day is great for the butt muscles." I patted my behind.

A chuckle sounded behind me. I turned my head and saw a male doctor following us. In my haste I hadn't heard his footsteps. Heat seeped into my face. I climbed the steps faster.

Then I had to go to CCU to collect a blood gas. A fourteen-year-old girl lay in bed, a respirator protruding from her mouth. Her chest rose and fell with each pump of the machine. Eyes closed, she looked peaceful. Her face radiated innocence. Her light brown hair spread out on the pillow like a halo.

"What happened?" I asked the nurse in a whisper.

"She was at a party with her older sister. They were all drinking and then she went into the bathroom. When she didn't come out, her sister found her passed out on the floor. She wasn't breathing. She vomited but since she was unconscious, the vomitus choked her. Someone called 9-1-1. Then they did chest compressions but not mouth to mouth resuscitation."

"Circulating blood with no oxygen."

"Right. She's brain dead. We're just keeping her alive until they can harvest her organs."

Horribly sad. So young! I gazed at the beautiful teen for a minute before I could move. Then after shaking my head in disbelief and sighing deeply, I did my job.

As I was leaving, a middle-aged woman and another woman probably in her sixties—probably the mother and grandmother—walked in, arm-in-arm, clinging to each other. I'll never forget the desperate looks in their eyes. They stood at the bedside and held the girl's hands, just watching her, until someone would turn off the machine and they would lose their young girl forever.

I couldn't stop thinking about the pain in those women's faces. Unimaginable heartbreak. Amy had been fourteen just a few years ago. I had been lucky with her. Nothing horrible had happened to her in her teen years. What would I have done? My only child. I wondered if it was worse to lose your child if you only had one, or would it be just as bad to lose a child if you had ten of them? Probably the latter. Thank God I never had to find out.

I forced myself to shake off that depressing thought as the full moon brought more tragedy. "Blue Alert, ETA one minute" blared across the intercom—not much time. My heart did its usual racing when I heard those terrifying words and my stomach squeezed and sunk hard. I hated Blue Alerts. I'd never gotten used to them.

I ran down to the ER, donned all the required protective gear, and entered the room. A man in his twenties writhed on the bed, shouting, "Let me die!" Blood splattered everywhere—all over the patient's body. The red sticky fluid soaked the sheet and dripped onto the floor. Grateful for my protective booties, I sloshed through the blood to get to him.

A paramedic reported, "He shot himself. He has AIDS. A friend of his called 9-1-1." Consequently, professional duty dictated we try to save him.

Thick tension crackled in the crowded trauma room. I willed my hands to stop shaking. No one liked to work around AIDS-infected blood. In spite of that, our trauma crew bustled around in professional synchronicity. One nurse started an IV. The lab aide drew venous blood for standard trauma testing. Another nurse took vital signs. Two X-ray techs shot X-rays with a portable machine. A different nurse jotted down notes.

My job involved inserting a needle into a pumping artery and withdrawing the patient's arterial blood to analyze for pH, oxygen, and carbon-dioxide levels. It was a challenge I usually relished, however not on a Blue-Alert AIDS patient. He flailed his arms in near-hysteria.

"I HAVE TO POKE YOU WITH A NEEDLE IN YOUR WRIST," I shouted. He stared at me, panic showing in his eyes. "HOLD STILL!"

This was a worst-case scenario for me. AIDS patient. Writhing. Needle. AIDS-filled blood everywhere.

With my left hand, I grabbed and held his arm to keep it steady, rendering me unable to feel for a pulse. Holding the needle in my right hand, I blindly jabbed him in his wrist. I prayed my years of experience would guide me to that artery without the benefit of feeling for it and that I wouldn't poke myself. God must have heard my plea because I got it without a problem.

I got out of there as soon as I could. Leaning against the trauma room door, I examined the blue paper booties protecting my shoes. Spots of bright-red blood splattered over the tops. With my gloved hands, I carefully removed the booties, folded them inside out then discarded them along with my gloves in an infectious waste can.

I pulled the blue paper bonnet off my head and shook out my hair. Then I peeled off my outer paper gown and mask and threw them all away. After a quick glimpse at the rest of the trauma team working selflessly on the Blue-Alert patient, I placed the sample I'd drawn into a cup of crushed ice. With rubber gloves still on, I rushed down the hallway back to the lab. Now that I was out of the trauma room, feelings of pride to be part of that team rushed through me.

After returning to the lab, I analyzed the arterial blood sample. Everyone had their specific task to do. Blood bank readied blood to be given to the Blue Alert patient if necessary. Chemistry department spun venous blood samples for their specified Blue Alert panel of tests. The hematology department quickly did their cell counts.

One hour later, "Blue Alert ETA three minutes" blared again. This time the patient was a large female in her fifties, drunk, screaming and writhing. Car accident. A big woman, she was probably one and a-half times my size. "I HAVE TO POKE YOU WITH A NEEDLE IN YOUR WRIST," I shouted. "HOLD STILL!"

But she was too drunk to cooperate. Her strong arm was too much for me. Sure enough, her flailing arm swatted me and I poked myself with my needle. Thank God I hadn't poked her yet and the needle hadn't been contaminated. Seemed like I was doing a lot of thanking God that night. The needle went right through my glove and drew blood. Cursing to myself, I pulled on another glove, got a new sterile needle and tried again. Everyone else was too busy with their own duties to help me. This time I got in and out successfully without poking myself and left.

The "what-ifs" filled my head. What if she had knocked my hand *after* I had poked her and the needle was contaminated and she had AIDS? What if I had poked myself after drawing that male AIDS patient?

A nurse-friend of mine had done just that once—started an IV on an AIDS patient and then accidentally poked herself. She was undergoing a series of shots to help prevent her body from contracting the disease and she never did. The potential dangers of my job made me even more nervous to go to Blue Alerts.

I thought of the people I worked with in that Blue Alert room. Trauma surgeon, ER doctor, multiple nurses, two x-ray techs, a lab aide, a paramedic and myself. Sometimes I hear the public complain of the high-cost of medical care but did they ever think of the skills, the education, the selfless dedication of medical teams who risk their own health to help others? We deserved decent salaries.

***

Sick of Phoenix heat, Mike and I slipped away to San

Francisco for vacation. Friends who'd visited there in the past told me to bring lots of warm, bulky sweaters. So I did. I looked forward to enjoying hot coffee on cool days. I longed to experience crisp air.

But that October, the San Francisco area experienced record high heat. Sweat dripped down my face onto my bulky sweaters. I hadn't brought anything else. We went to Chinatown and purchased a bunch of T-shirts. But even in T-shirts and jeans, we baked under the burning sun while crossing over the Bay to Alcatraz with nowhere to find shade.

The record high heat caused destructive fires in the area. Or was it the other way around? The fires destroyed many homes so I couldn't complain about a little heat. We loved it there and visited vineyards and redwood forests and vowed to get back there someday to hopefully enjoy their famous cool weather!

Meanwhile, Amy was still dating that nice guy her own age who worked as a plumber. After he proposed and she accepted, Amy and I went to Barnes and Noble and gathered some books on planning weddings. Then we sat at a table drinking coffee and chose which books we wished to purchase.

In 1995 they married. My little girl. Her whole life flashed before my eyes as I watched her standing in front of the church. A beautiful bride. It's difficult in today's world, I believe, to meet a nice person with whom to share your life. Someone who will think even your footprint in powder is precious. It was a relief that Amy found that special someone. I squeezed Mike's hand, happy to have him next to me, sharing life's moments. Life was good.

***

One day I was talking to another tech and I said, "Blue Alerts make me so nervous. I hate them, even though I may feel good when I do a good job."

She said, "I feel like I'm in my element when I go there."

There is a type of personality who thrives on the excitement and tension of emergencies. Fortunately there are people like that. Unfortunately, I wasn't one of those people. I did not feel in my element at all.

Yes, I needed to be challenged at work or I would get bored, but the fast-pace of a life-and-death trauma center made me dread going to work no matter what department I worked in, but especially when I was assigned to blood gases. Perhaps it was because I was getting older and just wanted to slow down a bit. I liked the patient contact but not in a trauma setting.

A graveyard tech had just become a grandmother and requested a few days off to be with her daughter and new grandchild. The lab said no. It was busy and they were short-staffed, so this woman couldn't even get time off to help her daughter.

Hearing that upset me but didn't surprise me. The previous January I had requested a Monday off for that upcoming June. That particular weekend, Monday would fall after my weekend off and I wanted to attend a three-day women's Church Retreat in Prescott, Arizona.

"Sorry," my chemistry supervisor had said, "someone else has already requested that week off and we'll be short-staffed."

Evidently even requesting one lousy day off, six months ahead of time, wasn't early enough. Disappointed, I didn't register for the women's retreat. I had really wanted to go but I shrugged it off because, aside from the tension of Blue Alerts, I essentially liked my job and sacrifices came with it.

When Monday of that particular June weekend finally came, I was scheduled 9:30 a.m. to 6:00 p.m. in chemistry. I got out of bed at 8:00 a.m., got ready for work and as I was leaving my house at 9:00 a.m., the phone rang. It was the big boss at the lab. "We're slow today and there's not much on the schedule for the rest of the day. Do you mind not coming in to work today?"

Cancelling someone out or sending someone home on slow days was common procedure in the lab. It happened a lot in the summertime when many people fled our hot valley and the hospital census dropped.

So I didn't go to work that day. The same day I had requested off six months earlier for the retreat but had been turned down. No work. No retreat either. I claimed eight vacation hours so my paycheck wouldn't suffer but irritation seethed inside me. I began to question if the sacrifices were really worth it anymore.

I'd passed through various phases during my twenty-year career. Initially I went into the medical field because the subject matter fascinated me. Gradually, however, the reasons changed. I reflected on why I loved this job so much.

I liked the mental stimulation, the challenges requiring skills and experience, the rush one got from doing a stressful job well, the knowledge we were helping people. Over the years, I'd worked with blood, urine and feces and had also tested gastric juice, kidney stones, ear drainage, eye goop, semen, nasal drainage, penis discharge, vaginal swipings, spinal fluid, wounds, pus. Basically, anything that comes out of the body, we test it. Oh, how fun. When looked at in a purely scientific manner, it really is fascinating and one gets used to it. I suppose humans can get used to almost anything if we have to.

I thought about my crazy career. I needed to weigh the pros against the cons. Now that I was working behind the sanctuary of four walls most of the time, I felt frequently isolated from medical personnel in other departments and the patients.

All of us could be doing something else with our lives. Sick people cough in our faces. Lab and nurses work with needles, sometimes poking ourselves accidentally. X-ray techs expose themselves to potentially dangerous rays every day. Respiratory therapists work with sputum and spit while their patients struggle to take another breath. We risk our health every day. The stress is high and the money is average.

So why do we do it? Perhaps it's the thrill of saving lives. It's a rush you get, leaving you on an endorphin-induced high. Some people tell me they thrive on the fast action of emergencies and get bored with anything less exciting—trauma junkies. There's a brother/sisterhood among medical staff, a shared camaraderie like a secret club. Or maybe it's the feeling of being needed or the joy of taking care of others. And of course there's the job stability. People will always get sick. For whatever reason, we're all here because it fulfills something inside of us.

But was I getting to a point in my life when the stress was getting to be too much?

***

Amy came into the lab one late 1996 evening when I was scheduled in chemistry. She was beaming. "We think we might be pregnant. I need to do a pregnancy test."

I knew they wanted a baby. They had been married over a year so I wasn't shocked but I wasn't prepared for the emotions that stormed through me when I saw the positive result pop up. Disbelief.

How could I not believe it? Of course it was true. But my little girl having a baby? Where had all those years gone? I was too young to be a grandma! Wasn't mid-to-late-forties too young for this? When I got used to the idea, however, I looked forward to this new phase of my life.

In the summer of 1997, my daughter went into labor with my first grandchild. I went to the hospital to be with her and my son-in-law. Things were done differently than twenty-eight years prior. I remembered a labor room back in 1969, being wheeled in and transferred to another bed in the delivery room while in a haze of pain, then recuperating in a different recovery room before being moved to my regular room for eight days and three roommates in succession while healing from the difficult delivery. I prayed my daughter wouldn't have the problems I did.

There was worry of some kind for the baby and the doctor ordered an ultrasound while Amy was in labor. The results looked good, fortunately. Then I sat with her and my son-in-law in the labor room, having no idea that same room would become the delivery room and the recovery room all-in-one.

I hadn't planned on staying for the delivery but things happened fast. They injected a shot into her spinal cord and the pain stopped immediately. Thank God. It hadn't been that way for me at all.

Then she started pushing the baby out. "Get the camera!" she shouted to me.

I rummaged through her purse and found it, then handed it to my son-in-law who looked like he was in a daze of panic. His eyes bugged open as he examined the camera. "How do I do this?" he asked.

As Amy pushed again, she screamed, "Give it to Mother!"

He passed the camera to me with a look of relief on his face. I hadn't brought my reading glasses, not having planned on reading anything. I couldn't see what those tiny buttons on the camera were for and had no idea which one to push. "I can't see. What do I do?"

201

After another hard push, Amy threw me an exasperated look. "Oh, give it to me!" She grabbed the camera out of my hand and snapped some pictures herself of the baby's head which was out by this time.

My son-in-law and I gave each other sheepish looks. The entire situation felt surreal to me.

Amy tossed the camera back to me and resumed pushing. Finally the rest of the baby entered the world.

A girl! A beautiful, healthy little girl!

There were two nurses in the room and the doctor. One nurse grabbed my granddaughter and tended to her while the other nurse and the doctor tended to Amy.

I was elated the baby was a girl. Hallelujah! I only had one child and having a daughter had been so much fun that I couldn't imagine anything else as precious. I wouldn't experience for a couple more years how precious little boys were, too.

The nurse checked out the baby, weighed her, six pounds fifteen ounces, wrapped her in a blanket and handed her to my daughter. When it was eventually my turn to hold the baby, I looked into her little face and thanked God.

She was very alert. Her eyes looked around at everything, as if in deep thought wondering, *What is all this?* She appeared different than Amy did as a baby. Amy had a fat round dark-red face topped with thick black hair. The cutest baby in the hospital. None other could compare. She grew to be blonde with green eyes and light complexion.

And now this baby, although smaller with less hair, was most certainly the cutest baby in this hospital. Probably the world!

Everyone was healthy and in a couple days went home. I was lucky this had all happened on my day off. As I held my granddaughter and looked into her sweet face, I started thinking about my career. All those years in the medical field working weekends, days, evenings, graveyards, holidays including Christmas, Christmas Eve, Thanksgiving. Missing all those big occasions with my daughter and scrambling to get a day off here and there. The years had passed too quickly. I didn't want to miss anything anymore. I didn't want it to be that way as a grandmother. When Amy was young, I hadn't had a choice—I had to work. But now I reevaluated my needs. Mike and I weren't rich but he had a steady paycheck, we had some money saved, our bills were paid off, money in retirement, and we could afford a small drop in my salary if I reduced my hours a little.

I felt like I was moving into a new phase of life.

First I asked if I could go part-time at work but they were too busy and needed me to fill my fulltime hours so they said no. I didn't know what to do.

After a night of tossing and turning in bed trying to decide what to do, I threw off my covers and went to work. It was crazy there. It must have been a full moon because everything went wrong. I couldn't find where the standards were kept. I searched all over and couldn't locate them. The doctor had ordered a slew of tests on a patient and I couldn't remember how to run one of the machines. None of the reagents I needed had been reconstituted, nor the controls. I had to find the standards, reconstitute the reagents and the controls, flush out and prime the Coulter Counter, and figure out how to run the chemistry machines. I was way behind and the doctor came in complaining that it was taking too long. I didn't know what to do. My heart pounded with fear and my palms were all sweaty.

Then I woke up in a panic, my bed-covers on the floor. Another nightmare. I'd been having many of those lately.

Over the next few weeks I thought a lot about my career and what I wanted now that I was pushing fifty and a grandma. I loved science and loved kids. I wanted a normal schedule so I could have time to be a grandma. I talked with Mike and he was supportive of my switching careers. My work was interesting, challenging, and I liked my co-workers and I had developed many skills over the years. But I felt it was time to move on. I had worked almost twenty years in the medical field.

I took some required education courses over the next couple years on my days off and got a teaching certificate. To my never-ending surprise, I obtained a teaching position after my first interview as a high school science teacher in an alternative school for at-risk students. It turned out to be a whole lot more work than I ever could have imagined, but I loved it and it gave me a normal schedule. I grew to love teaching also and loved my students.

Leaving the medical field proved emotionally more difficult than I expected. After twenty years in one field, I felt a deep loyalty. The break-away burdened my heart, so I stayed on as an "on-call" technologist, filling in on occasional weekends, holidays—but not Christmas or Thanksgiving!—and summer vacations. I enjoyed seeing my lab friends. I had missed them and working with them again was fun, hardly like work at all. But after one year of the extra hours I came to my senses and made the final break and quit altogether. The transition was now complete.

The nightmares continued for years. Despite the obvious deep-seated fears I evidently had, I missed many aspects of working in a medical laboratory and will always admire my fellow lab technologists and other healthcare professionals for their dedication and skills.

Years ago I had searched for my professional passion. That search led me to the medical field. It had provided me with a decent income and fulfillment. Being a mother also brought me much joy. I had raised my daughter alone for many years and she became a lovely woman. Now it was time to pass the torch, both personally and professionally, and enter a new phase of life.

I love being a wife to Mike, a mother, and a grandma. Three now—one girl and two boys. As I look back on my life, I realize that as I kept my trust in God, everything turned out all right, no matter what challenges I faced along the way. God always took care of us.

Sometimes I'm so happy that my joy keeps me awake at night. And I thank God for my many blessings.

Life is good.

The End

Amy and me

Mike and me

Amy on her wedding day

Me with my three grandchildren

Thank you for sharing this experience with me. I hope God has blessed you in many ways, also.

To read about my experiences teaching science in an inner-city high school, read "*No Child Left Behind??? The true story of a teacher's quest*" by Elizabeth Blake, an award-winning book found on Amazon and on Kindle.

17029832R00122

Made in the USA
San Bernardino, CA
28 November 2014